THE BLACK BELT
HOW TO DO KARATE

The Art Of Personal Self-Defense

Written By Hachidan Master John McGee

Edited By Burt Anderson

Forward
By: Great Grand Master Aaron Banks

Amazon Paperback Books, First Edition,
ISBN# 978-1-893257-73-3

Every effort has been made to make this book as
complete and accurate as possible. However, there
may be mistakes in typography or content. Also, this
book contains information on martial arts only up to
the original copyright date. Therefore this book should

DEDICATIONS

BY THE AUTHOR

Dedicated to my wife, Jane and my mother, Mary. Though they have left this plane of existence, in my heart these wonderful ladies will always be alive and by my side.

My deepest gratitude to my karate mentor Grand Master Aaron Banks.

My deep gratitude to my karate teacher, Grand Master Shigeru Numano, who first showed me the way of the martial arts.

My deep appreciation to my Iaido teacher, Grand Master Yoshiteru Otani, the highest ranking all-around martial artist in the world, who lighted my pathway to martial arts knowledge.

My heartfelt thanks to Carol Lee for her help. She is a true patroness of the arts.

My heartfelt thanks to my writing teacher, Professor Walter James Miller of New York University, who showed me how to achieve structure, style and syntax in my work.

My sincere gratitude to Sidney Porcelain, a writing instructor, who was among the first to guide my pen.

My thanks to my students of the past, present and future.

My thanks also to Dennis Harkins, William Wong, Leonard Tusa, Shawn Roberts, David Olivieri, Russel Antonucci, Christopher Androulakis, Al Vaughn, Scott Leonardi, Mark Wise, Michael Zuckerberg, Stephen B. Shedden, Howard Portney, Stephen Fahy, Robert Robinson, Paul Fay, James Anderson, David Brown, Scott Silverman, and Tom Scroth.

And to my many comrades and friends in and out of the Martial Arts World, too numerous to mention, my thanks and gratitude for your help and support throughout the years.

BY THE EDITOR

Dedicated to Carol Lee Metzger, in whose care John McGee placed this manuscript for future publication, and who entrusted me with its publication.

My deepest thanks to John McGee's mentor Great Grand Master Aaron Banks who was kind enough to write a Forward for this book.

And to my loving wife Melanie whose patience and love allowed me the time and space to edit and bring this book to life.

CONTENTS

FORWARD

It was 1967. I was conducting a martial-arts competition at Manhattan Center on 34th Street in New York City. A huge gentleman with flaming red hair and a red beard approached me. He was carrying a large stick, and for a moment I imagined that, had he been wearing an eye patch, he had just come from a casting call for a pirate movie! "Hi! I'm John McGee", he said in a gentle voice that bespoke his impressive physical presence. "I'm a writer."

Fast forward a dozen years. John McGee, my lady friend Janet and I were seated in a Chinese restaurant on Mott Street having a leisurely discussion about my upcoming martial arts event at Madison Square Garden. John casually asked: "Would you do me a big favor?" "Of course John, what can I do for you". "I want to do something really spectacular for your audience." Then, in a matter of fact tone he said: "I want to commit Hara-Kiri on stage in front of 20,000 people." "You're not serious", I replied, though knowing John I feared he might be. "Yes, I really am. It's an honorable way to die. My greatest desire is to go out in a blaze of glory in front of a large audience". Of course, I said "**No!**".

John protested that he would have an assistant with a basket ready to catch his guts as they fell from his slashed belly, and a blanket to shield the audience from the site of gore and blood. I was able to convince him that, if for no other reason, the legal implications of including this act of suicide in my show might be a bit harsh on my future career as the greatest martial-arts promoter of the day. We left it at that. I'm not certain that my lady friend ever recovered her composure after listening to this dialog!

Three months later, 8th Degree Black Belt, Master John T. McGee, swallowed over a hundred sleeping pills and never awoke. We buried him on Staten Island, together at last with his dearly beloved wife Jane.

For the twelve years between these incidents, "Big John", as he was affectionately known, proved himself not only to be a master practitioner of the martial arts, but also the finest reporter of martial-arts events that ever lived. In everything he wrote he was straight forward and honest. He never favored anyone. He did an A to Z full-detailed blast of a story on every event. He captured every detail of every move, and did so in a way such that the lay reader could understand the nuances of the fighting arts.

As a freelance writer, John wrote for every martial arts magazine of the day, most of which no longer exist. He wrote for *Black Belt* when it was under the care of late editor Mito Yuhara and was the premier martial arts publication of its time. He wrote for the fine *Inside Kung Fu.* His articles were featured in renowned bodybuilder Dan Lurie's *World Karate Magazine, Tae Kwon Do Times, Official Karate, Oriental Fighting Arts* and *Action Magazine,* as well as many mainstream publications. In 1974 and 1975 he was honored by The World Karate Hall of Fame.

He was an honest, ethical human being, who desperately wanted the public to understand the mental side of the martial arts as well as the physical. <u>I would vouch for John one million percent!</u> He truly understood all aspects the martial arts. A rare combination of Master martial arts practitioner and expert writer, he could project what he was writing so the reader could actually feel present at the events of which he wrote so eloquently.

John worked on the manuscript for this book over a number of years. He was frustrated and deeply disappointed at having never been able to interest a major publisher simply because he was too honest and blunt in his portrayal of the fighting arts. I cannot imagine any reader of *The Black Belt – How To Do Karate* not coming away with an appreciation of John's purest intentions, as well as a basic understanding of the life-saving art of personal self-defense.

John's greatest and deepest loves were for his mom (whose toughness as a boxer herself kept John in his place!), and his dearly beloved wife and writing-partner Jane. Shortly after his mom died Jane was diagnosed with terminal cancer. She died shortly thereafter , far,

far too young. John was totally devastated. All of the light had gone out of his life. He was never the same. It was not long thereafter that we had that fateful Chinese dinner, followed by his untimely death a few short months later.

It is my greatest hope that this book will serve to perpetuate the legacy of this truly fine and dedicated practitioner of American martial arts. May he finally rest in peace.

Great Grand Master Aaron Banks

New York City, August 2012

FORWARD BY THE EDITOR

In 1979 a dear friend of mine, Carol Lee, told me of a close friend of hers who had recently passed away. John McGee apparently was so devastated by the untimely death of his wife and the passing of his mother, and the rejection by potential publishers of the martial arts book he had written, that for reasons few could fully understand he decided to take his own life in 1977.

I was writing and self-publishing at the time, and Carol asked me whether I had any interest in the manuscript. Apparently it had been rejected by all of the major publishing houses as being "too controversial". I said I would enjoy publishing it when I could, and decided to copyright the book at that time. Shortly thereafter I unfortunately was badly disabled with multiple sclerosis. Publishing and writing took a back seat to my full recovery, which at the time seemed totally unlikely to my doctors.

It is now thirty-three years later. Over the years, through the intervention of European physicians, my MS magically (according to my U.S. doctors, it had to be magic) was cured! I'm 75, walk with a cane, but otherwise expect to live forever! Carol married, I married, and John's manuscript was more or less forgotten, though it followed me around packed safely in a box through a number of worldwide moves.

Carol and I communicated over the years, but lived at far different ends of the country and never had any personal contact other than exchanging Christmas cards. I knew nothing at all about John McGee. Had he been named John Won-Fong I might have looked into his karate background more seriously. Somehow an Irishman throwing spinning kicks didn't compute!

Recently I wrote and published a book about the so-called Mayan Calendar End of Time. I decided to send out proof copies to old friends who I thought might find it interesting, Carol Lee (now

Metzger) being one of them. After receiving it she called me, and we chatted for the first time in many years. (She had found a glaring technical error in my new book! Thanks Carol, I think.)

We talked about John's book, and she said how much she felt that John, and she, would love to have it published. Somewhat out of guilt I decided that I would immediately look into doing so.

I know very little about karate. Aside from Chuck Norris, Bruce Lee, and *The Karate Kid*, I've always been clueless. For all I knew John McGee was just some guy who fancied himself a karate dude and really didn't know squat. I decided to look up some of the individuals to whom he dedicated the work, fully expecting that they had all since died of old age.

I started by doing a Google search for "Master Aaron Banks", the "mentor" John thanked in his dedication. I was pretty shocked when I read Bank's lengthy Wikipedia bio! He is now "Great

Grand Master Aaron Banks", apparently the most famous martial arts practitioner and promoter that ever lived! I have never heard of any other **"Great"** Grand Master, so I was duly impressed.

A Google search turned up the website of a karate organization headed by Great Grand Master Banks. I called the listed phone number, and left a brief message. Essentially I wanted to see whether he even knew or remembered one "John McGee". About an hour later I was rather surprised and honored to receive a phone call directly from the Great Grand Master himself!

We talked for almost two hours. It was one of the most enjoyable conversations I can ever remember having with anyone! What an incredible, and humble, individual. I think because we are both New Yorkers, he from the Bronx and I from Brooklyn, we spoke as kindred spirits. I really hope to meet him some day. Amazing man, now 84, and still actively promoting World

Championship martial arts competitions! May he live long and prosper.

About half of our long conversation centered around Master John McGee. Much to my relief as a publisher, McGee turned out to be the "real deal". Aside from being an 8th Degree Black Belt (known as a Hachidan) and highly-respected teacher of the martial arts, John was considered to be the single most respected freelance martial arts writer of his time. **"I'd vouch for John 1000%"** related Great Grand Master Banks. He then went on to tell me of the years that he and John travelled together to competitions all around the country, and how accurately John could report on the many nuances of the sport.

John was apparently a very famous reporter in his time, writing for every major karate magazine (Black Belt, Inside Kung Fu, Oriental Fighting Arts, Official Karate, and others) and was also widely published outside of that realm. He also ran his own karate training academy, and was a respected acupressure practitioner (Shiatsu) as well.

Needless to say I suddenly felt a sense of urgency about getting McGee's book published! At the time I originally received the manuscript, as a self-publisher I would have had to print a few thousand copies at enormous expense, and then literally go door to door to book stores to market it. This process, which I had gone through with other books prior to that time, was expensive, and frustrating. It was always impossible to compete with the big publishing houses, or to interest thousands of libraries in shelving a single self-published book. Aside from the love of writing and the considerable ego trip of seeing one's name on a book cover, it was a really good thing my wife had a real job!

Things today are **TOTALLY** different. (Though thankfully my wife **still** has a real job!) This is the Golden Age of the self-publisher! Through Amazon's

Kindle Direct Publishing platform and Amazon's Create Space paperback-book-on-demand platform, (and all of the electronic book reading devices available such as Nook and iPads, Sony and others, available through Smashwords), it is possible for an independent ("Indie") publisher to reach an audience of hundreds of millions worldwide at ZERO cost, and virtually overnight!

I originally was given this manuscript totally "shuffled" without any page numbers or chapter order whatsoever. The chapter titles are mine. The order of presentation is mine, as are the Appendices, Glossary, this Forward, my Dedication and the fanciful cover design. Plus, of course, the wonderful Forward by Great Grand Master Aaron Banks. Other than that, the text is essentially exactly as written decades ago by Master John McGee.

It should also be noted that the original book was intended to have photographs, which Master McGee credited to John Holland Duer and David Wong. Unfortunately these photos were not originally given to me with the manuscript and cannot be located.

And so, sometime in late August 2012, the late Master John McGee and Carol Lee Metzger will realize their dream of seeing John's **timeless book** published. Damn sorry it took me so long. We plan to find a worthy American martial arts charity or organization to which to donate in John's honor a substantial part of any net profits we might realize.

In editing and creating the electronic manuscript of this book over many months I made an effort to personally understand the many self-defense techniques McGee describes in detail. Simply **reading** descriptions of the techniques did very little for my confidence that I could actually apply any of them if I needed to do so in a real-life confrontation. <u>That changed when I enlisted the aid of two friends of mine who were equally curious about real-life self-defense.</u>

After literally going through each and every move in the book together in <u>slow motion</u> the wisdom and art of each move became totally apparent! It was quite clear to us that this book could teach **anyone**, even someone as karate-clueless as I, to protect themselves in any threatening confrontation. <u>**The key is to practice in slow motion with another person, and repeat, and practice, and repeat again, until the moves described in McGee's words become physical reflex.**</u>

Remember, there is no substitute for actual full-speed contact- training under the guidance of trained professional practitioners.

I believe that **anyone** in the general public will find this book both entertaining and useful, whether or not learning karate in itself is of any interest. In fact, it could very well be a life-saver!

More important, I am convinced that the material in this book will be of great value to anyone first beginning to become truly interested in learning or perfecting their martial arts skills.

I also believe very strongly that even experienced practitioners at **any** level will find Master McGee's obvious depth of knowledge of martial arts and especially his depth of **practical-wisdom** to be of real value in their own pursuit of perfection.

And if this book helps save a life or two along the way Master John McGee's original purpose will be fulfilled.

Burt Anderson, Amado, Arizona
August 2012

CHAPTER ONE

<u>PRACTICAL SELF-DEFENSE</u>

My initial exposure to the martial arts began with a self-defense course at my local YMCA. However, a friend and I who had signed up for the course became disillusioned after we discovered that the instructor didn't have any idea how to stop an assailant if he attacked with a knife in an underhand thrust.

In over a quarter of a century of martial arts training my own experience has led me to the conclusion that too often flashy but useless theatrical techniques are substituted for more mundane moves that would effectively save the student's life in an actual confrontation. This happens not because the instructors or authors of martial arts books are con men but because Americans will not in general pay for the obvious. They prefer the mysterious or obscure.

My personal self-defense odyssey began when, as a scared kid from the ghetto who was raised on carnivals, circuses and migrant labor camps, I decided to learn how to survive. In the years since then my search for the principles of self-defense has been fruitful. All of what I have learned I have tried to pass on in this book.

My teacher, Master Shigeru Numano, told me the following a long time ago. In essence his message was flexible, both mentally and physically. A lack of versatility is what I've found sadly lacking in so many books on self-defense.

Master Numono: "My techniques are determined by the opponent's weakness and size. A foot sweep is good against somebody who does not have good balance. That is why it is effective against a big person; his center of balance is higher than mine. But a tall man who is also heavy presents a problem. He may be so heavy that it is like attempting to foot sweep the Empire

State Building." Master Numano shook his head: "Very difficult."

"You may have noticed that I have not mentioned flying kicks. I don't believe in them. Yes, I know that most smaller men go flying through the air. I consider this ridiculous in the context of a fighting art. It's great for the movies, TV, or the covers of a magazine. In other words, it's strictly for show. Once a man has left the ground he is completely helpless. Any good karateka can knock him out of the air with a block. Man is not a bird and should not try to fight like one."

"I prefer 'sacrifice' techniques – throwing a reverse punch then dropping to the floor and throwing a side kick. That's very effective against a larger man. However, not everyone should use sacrifice techniques. Big men are just too slow for them. Put it like this: an army attacking a castle needs three times as many soldiers as the defenders have if they are going to succeed in capturing the castle."

"My philosophy in fighting is an aggressive defense. Just standing there and blocking is no good. Any opponent will finally be able to score. The correct maneuver is to let the other fighter attack, and while he is wide open with no thoughts of defense a wise battler strikes **instantly** after he blocks. This I call an aggressive defense, the sure way to win in any real-life situation. Of course, it's not a strategy for a tournament fighter, but in a life-or-death situation it is definitely worthwhile."

Master Aaron Banks has said that the reverse punch and the front kick are the two most potent blows in karate. This is sound, practical reasoning.

The secret of mastering self-defense techniques is practice, practice, and more practice. If there is a school with Black Belt instructors in your area so much the better. In fact, I recommend that you make every effort to locate one. This book is not intended to replace the benefits of day-to-day instruction in a quality martial arts school. Rather, it should be regarded as a supplement to your fighting arts education.

A technique that students of mine have found particularly effective is: "No matter where you are, always try to be aware of when someone is behind you." Keep your own personal check list. When you are caught off guard, write "corpse" in the slot. When you know what's happening, enter "I'm alive". This simple procedure will help you to be aware of the world around you.

In karate there is a term called "Sanchin", meaning "three battles". It refers to the conflicts within a person of body, mind and spirit as they struggle to unify finally into a whole human being. The successfully integrated personality is imbued with self-confidence and inner calm. Such an individual is never a bully, nor does he or she necessarily accept every challenge. They are not obliged by their own insecurities to constantly reassure themselves of winning in a physical confrontation. This

<u>is the perfect description of a martial arts trained personality.</u>

Only you can insure your own survival through practical self-defense techniques. I truly believe that I have presented them in this book. Study the principles and adopt the techniques that work for you as your own. It could save your life.

CHAPTER TWO

<u>HOLLYWOOD HORSE POOP</u>

MOVIES AND THE MARTIAL ARTS

The tip of the assassin's blade touched the young girl's throat. She continued to hold a few grains of rice in her chopsticks, then, with a delicate gesture, she transferred them to her lips. She showed no concern. "I'm going to kill you!" the man hissed. Calmly, she placed the tip of her finger on the top of his sword, pushed, and sent him flying across the room. For added measure she took the sword from his broken hand and chopped off his head, thus showing how any properly reared young lady takes care of a dirty old masher!

At the same time, her blind boyfriend's foot finds the throat of another of the band of 50 that surrounds them. Holding hands, the boy and girl leap 50 feet into the air, their feet lashing out, bowling over opponents like tenpins.

They are twin cyclones cutting wide swaths of destruction through their enemies.

Most of the evil thugs still able to stand beat a hasty retreat, leaving their unconscious comrades behind. But a last contingent of eight of the assailants manages to corner the blind boy. Undaunted, he grasps the blade of one opponent, pulls it out of his hand and then decapitates all eight men with one swing that sends heads and spurting blood in all directions! Not to be outdone, the girl disarms an opponent and cuts off the legs of ten remaining men in two deft slashing motions.

This far-out Far East movie plot is true Women's Lib, although a spokesperson for the feminist organization calls martial arts movies "male rip-offs". Sexist or not, in movie houses across America martial arts movie adventures have driven westerns, that boast only two or three killings per reel, from the silver screen. In the wide assortment of Kung Fu, karate, or Japanese sword flicks,if one goes to the bathroom in the middle of the movie he is apt to miss 500 of the most gory killings imaginable. There is another ingredient common to all these films: the underdog always comes out on top!

If you think you've seen this all before, you have. These are stock-in-trade situations for most Asiatic movie companies. The Shaw Brothers, who produced the first Chinese "talkie" in 1926, crank out 40 movies per year. Sometimes there's only a slight change in cast, (or ketchup), from one gory production to another. Always there's the same trampoline to propel the heroes upward, making it appear as if they are jumping at least 100 feet in the air. Generally in these Chinese productions the good guys and gals are Chinese and the villains Japanese!

In the Land Of The Rising Sun, Japan, millions of fans swear by Toshiro Mifune, the fastest blade in the movies. Mifune has appeared in 100 epics of blood and thunder, though these

Western-Easterns passed unnoticed among America's theatregoers. Only "The *Seven Samurai*" won recognition, but Hollywood couldn't countenance the box-office receipts going to Japan, and turned out their own version (*The Magnificent Seven)* plus a sequel, both of which were actually just rootin' tootin' westerns!

Obviously, the Kung Fu techniques you see in such movies are completely unrealistic. If the viewer ever attempted to use them in a real fight he would of course be either injured or killed.

Why don't they show the real thing? Because movie and TV moguls are not martial arts men. Moreover, genuine techniques aren't always exciting to watch. Life and death struggles may even appear boring, except to the participants. In the early days of filmmaking, the Mexican hero Pancho Villa permitted some American cameramen to photograph one of his battles. Battle scenes had to be re-shot in the studio because the actual incidents were not dramatic enough! Some years ago in a newsreel theatre in New York City, two senators from a South American nation fought a real duel to the death with swords, but the film didn't generate one-tenth the excitement of Errol Flynn as Robinhood!

The late Bruce Lee did much to bring genuine martial arts techniques to movies and TV, for the simple reason that he was a superb practitioner. Although he did admit that his high kicks to the jaw as Kato in "*The Green Hornet*" series weren't practical in a real fight, they were used because they looked dramatic. In an actual bout he would have kept his kicks low, to the shin and groin, because it would have been easy to throw him off balance during those high kicks.

Bruce did get a touch of realism into *"The Green Hornet"* by being the first good guy to kick the villains where it hurt the most, though real-life fighters had been doing it for years, and many fights were decided simply by who did it first. Bruce Lee did it first on TV.

When he appeared as a guest on the *"Longstreet"* TV series, Bruce tried to get across to viewers the philosophy of Kung Fu and make them understand that there was much more to it than the chop-kick-kill-smash-in-the-face routine. Later in Hong Kong, he made history for both movies and the martial arts in a succession of films that are still pulling in crowds. Their success is deserved, for his work in these films remains the crowning achievement of a truly great artist.

Nudged by the growing interest in martial arts films and exhibits, ABC-TV decided it was time to try out a script that had been gathering dust for four years. *"Kung Fu"* made its debut as Movie of the Week. The ratings were not high, but the reviews were favorable and it was run again. This time *"Kung Fu"* was an overnight sensation! So was its star David Carradine, who found himself in a more demanding role than he'd bargained for. He had to actually **be** a Kung-Fu expert!

David Carradine freely admits and apologizes for the fact that he isn't Bruce Lee, who trained for years before his first TV break. Actually, there's no need for apologies. As soon as it became apparent that the show was a smash hit, Carradine began studying Kung Fu and the other martial arts, and he is now fully skilled. In addition, he has had the benefit of expert advice on the show. Master Kam Yuen, a high-ranking Chinese instructor, served as technical adviser and also had an acting part in the series. So the techniques used in the show were authentic, although David Carradine says that he suspects some of those weighty Oriental sayings came from *"Bartlett's Familiar Quotations"*!

To the credit of Hollywood let it be said that a couple of really stunning demonstrations of martial arts occurred in films made there many years ago. In the 1940's James Cagney made *"Blood*

On The Moon" and gave as fine a display of judo as you're likely to see anywhere. Of course Cagney happened to be a Third Degree Black Belt in judo!

Another movie featuring an excellent martial arts scene was *"The Manchurian Candidate",* made in 1962. Who will ever forget that memorable fight between Frank Sinatra and Henry Silva when they literally chopped up the place? Frank studied diligently for the scene, unfortunately to the point where he became over-confident and tried to break a board. He broke his hand instead!

In *"You Only Live Twice"* James Bond (007) gave audiences a real chance to see Oriental fighting arts in action, but unfortunately the techniques shown were not authentic. Later there was *"Melinda"* with some real karate people, including Jim Kelly. But from the standpoint of martial arts the movie was a nightmare. If any of those ersatz techniques were tried on the street the actors would be killed! In one horrible scene, a student challenged the karate instructor and beat him, yet still remained in the class. This simply wouldn't happen in real life.

Regarding the box office success of *"Melinda"*, director Hugh Roberts said: "I wanted to make a unique movie, something different from the typical action thriller, and I thought that by employing karate, the whole movie would appeal to the Black ethnic market because karate is a popular instrument – something with which they can identify. Karate helps the kids to have more self-esteem." That's probably as good a reason as any why Americans have taken martial arts movies to heart.

"Billy Jack", released in 1971, was the first motion picture to make serious use of a martial art. The plot was centered around a returning veteran of the Vietnam war. The hero, half-white and half-Indian, used the skills he learned in Viet Nam to protect himself from the racism of Americans at home. The movie won critical acclaim, and

introduced the Korean fighting art of Hapkido to American audiences.

How do actors rate as martial arts men? One instructor who has trained many stars said: "In general they're no good because they lack discipline and are on their own ego trips." He claims, however, that two of his students, Ben Gazzara and Clint Walker, have the right martial-arts spirit. Other instructors who have taught successful show people, such as Master Aaron Banks of the New York Karate Academy, concur.

The best karate practitioner in show business is Gregory Hines of "*Hines, Hines, and Dad*". Unfortunately he didn't snare the Bill Cosby role in "*I Spy*", or a part in any other of the punch and kick shows that would have demonstrated the outstanding karate expertise that made him a competitor of international reputation.

What are the effects of the martial arts movie explosion? One dramatic effect has been a surge of renewed interest in martial arts training, which is reflected in the expansion of many schools which were on the verge of closing down. Most instructors find, however, that as soon as some beginners realize that they won't become master killers in "10 easy lessons" they drop out!

On the negative side, the movies demonstrate the arts of cracking skulls and breaking necks with no thought to the suffering of the victim, and impressionable children and young adults may try to emulate the tactics of their movie heroes – with horrifying results.

Allen Roberts, a New York City public school teacher and Second Degree Black Belt in Korean karate, noted that he has personally seen children trying to imitate the ridiculous antics of movie fighting. Of course this tendency is by no means restricted to martial arts movies but is sadly true of movie violence in general.

Editor's Note: This book was written long before the unchecked insane violence of computer and internet "games", and the increasing violence portrayed on TV and in the movies. Is it any wonder why violence is so prevalent in our American society today?

CHAPTER THREE

THE MYTH OF THE SINGLE DEVASTATING BLOW

The big man's fist lashed out, nearly tearing his opponents head from his body. He picked up a second assailant and threw him over the cigarette machine. The third attacker was grabbed in a deadlock, and the giant ran his head into the bar. Now if this had been a movie the hero would have been kissed by the heroine and they would have driven off happily into the sunset.

Unfortunately for our real-life hero, Preston Carter, Sixth Degree karate Black Belt from New Jersey, the fight was just beginning. It had started in a bar in Trenton where Carter worked as a bouncer, and the men who had been knocked to the floor were unruly customers. One trouble-maker jumped to his feet and Carter knocked him down again with a reverse punch. (At karate tournaments Black Belt Carter had often broken eight slabs of concrete with one blow of his fist.) Another man bounced to his feet and charged; the Sixth Dan blasted out a side kick to the man's eye. But at that moment the Black Belt heard a sharp noise as a bullet from a .32 caliber revolver plowed into his upper back.

Carter spun around and his front kick smashed into one customer's groin. The karate-slayer shutoed one man to the ground, practically breaking his neck. A reverse punch lifted another attacker into the air but the man rose and Carter threw a bar stool toward him. Only then did Carter hear a woman screaming: "You've been shot!" Now his fury added new power to his defense. He pulled his own pistol and started firing at the three retreating figures. Although he emptied his revolver of six rounds he did not hit any of the fleeing culprits. Even now, with his adrenalin pumping less fiercely, Carter was not aware of having been shot.

Only when he bent down to pick up the bar stool he had thrown did he have an inkling of what had really happened. Suddenly jackknifed with pain, he collapsed. From that moment in 1972 Carter has not been able to walk and he will probably remain paralyzed for life. The damage from the bullet has made him a paraplegic.

Six months before that crippling tragedy he had been dining in a restaurant when a fellow karate instructor challenged him to fight. Carter begged off, but when the man came at him with a knife he flattened him with a reverse punch and a front kick. Then Carter, who has always been thought of as "The Gentle Giant" by his friends, turned around to walk away and avoid trouble. The man reached out, grabbed Carter's legs and began to slash at him. The Black Belt now turned and went to work on the knifer. It took 50 stitches to sew up the cuts in Carter's legs and 287 stitches for his assailant's face!

In retrospect the Sixth Dan made two mistakes in these incidents, which he readily admits. But they were errors in judgment. I'll have more to say about self-defense and the law in Chapter Eighteen, but to put the matter simply if Carter had fought to kill from the beginning the results would have been quite different. Thus, what happened to Preston Carter was the result of wrong decisions on his part, wrong decisions that were forced upon him by the law.

In a New England State, a Sensei who worked as a bouncer in a bar killed an unruly customer. The karate instructor will shortly stand trial for murder. Carter himself faced trial on the charge of knocking out the eye of one of his attackers.

We asked Carter, if he could turn back the clock and know what he knows today, what would he have done? He answered sadly: "I would have made sure the man was unable to attack me, even if it meant breaking both his arms, in the case of the man with the knife. If I had it to do all over again and a man came at me with a weapon, I would kill him. And the same thing goes for those three guys. If two men attack you, even if they are unarmed, go in to kill them! It's kill or be killed on the streets nowadays. That's what I tell my students. Even if they go to jail, it's better than ending up the way I am. Hell, I'm in jail for the rest of my life anyway!"

"It used to be different years ago." Carter shook his head in bafflement. "Then, if you got into a fight, you would hit a man and he would fall down and that would be the end of it as you walked away. I never tried to hurt a man or disfigure him. Just knock him down and that would be the end of the fight. But nowadays it's different. Everybody's a jitterbug (troublemaker). I still say that a Black Belt shouldn't carry weapons because it's against the law. But if he is attacked and there is any sort of weapon handy, he should most certainly use it."

Good advice from a man who learned a bitter lesson the hard way. But Carter's tragedy teaches another lesson as well. At the time of this incident Preston Carter was stronger and far more knowledgeable about fighting than the average man. Yet his blows were certainly not the all-devastating ones the entertainment world have led us to expect from karate. I noticed this gap between myth and reality at the first full-contact karate bouts I ever witnessed. (Before this time karate matches were of the "blows-pulled" variety.)

Many of the gentlemen hadn't had a real fight since grammar school and believed, until they discovered otherwise, that their single blows were powerful enough to stop tanks! Amazement turned to horror as player after player threw full-focused kicks to little avail. One could hear the sounds of contact all over the place but the guy who got kicked didn't even blink, and our heroes suddenly realized they weren't the lethal weapons they'd thought!

Then one guy would wrestle the other and land on top of the V.I.P.s on the stage, or crash into the audience. Weight means a lot in catch-as-catch-can wrestling!

In most **no-contact** tournaments it is not unusual for a few jaws and noses to be broken. At this **full-contact** show there wasn't even a loose tooth! Now this brings up an interesting point. When players are concentrating on **form** their blows are more powerful than when they forget techniques.

Undoubtedly poor conditioning had a lot to do with the dismal showing, but one fact stands out above all others: <u>**Karate is not a secret cult of the single deadly blow.**</u>

CHAPTER FOUR
YOUR FOUNDATION
THE STANCE

It is important to know when a stance helps, and when it does not. There is a good reason why one should not necessarily go into a karate stance at the first sign of trouble.

Once I was witness to a dispute between two drivers. One was a big burly American, an aggressive obnoxious type. The other was a diminutive Japanese gentleman. The man from Japan kept trying to entice the big mouth into a deserted building where they could settle their differences in private. The angry American, confident in his poundage security-advantage, agreed and followed him in. I recognized the Japanese gentleman as a Fifth Dan Black Belt.

The reader should not be surprised at the outcome of this encounter. Suffice it to say that the American had been aware of his opponent's credentials he would never have let himself be tricked into his downfall. The lesson to be learned here is that a good martial artist does not ballyhoo his strength as if he were an attraction at a carnival. He walks with humble mien and uses his special skill only when required. In fact, many times the true martial artist need not give a demonstration of his physical skill in order to command respect. It is the quiet authority of his tone, the "I-will-brook-no-nonsense" voice, that carries the day.

Now that I have given an example of when not to use form, here is the other side of the coin:

Sometimes just getting into a stance can be as effective as the flashing of a weapon. The time was 2:00 A.M., and the scene was a lower East Side New York street. I had been glancing idly at a display poster when suddenly I heard voices behind me. Turning quickly I saw three tough looking youths walking in my direction.

Sensing danger, I broke into a fast trot and managed to reach a corner fruit stand. There, on the pathway to the store proper, and with mountains of boxes on both sides of me and my back protected by the entrance, I went into a back stance and shouted a very loud "Kia!". The teenagers took one look at me in my karate stance ready to give battle and were so taken aback that they ran away!

Now this incident occurred a number of years ago when the martial arts craze was zooming to new heights of popularity. People half believed that fighting techniques from the Orient possessed some magical power. That same maneuver would very likely fail today as a deterrent because many of the postures of karate have been shown to be inadequate in full-contact bouts.

Perhaps some readers will be familiar with the story of the man in the sports car who is cut off by a truck. The sports car driver, a little guy, jumps out of his fancy automobile, gets into a karate stance, and screams: "Karate!". The truck driver hits him over the head with a wrench and yells: "Monkey wrench!". The point here is that while a conspicuous display of karate prowess can be helpful, it is not always foolproof.

I know of one youngster from a tough neighborhood who read a karate book, managed to break a board, and then put on a Superman cape and went around to the school yard to boast of his powers. The other lads soon showed him the error of his ways - - - - by slitting his throat.

This is obviously not a "nice white-upper-middle-class story". To be sure it's a world far removed from McGuffey's Reader, the Jim-throws-the-ball-and-John-catches-it   presentation of an American childhood. In a world where people are not obliged to cope with physical violence on an every-day basis in order to survive, and therefore are not of necessity discerning as to who is or is not likely to be dangerous, a loud yell and an aggressive stance will be impressive enough. But not in the ghetto world. In that harsh rougher world it takes more than loud noises and Superman capes to intimidate anyone.

Now let's take a look at the various basic karate stances:

BACK STANCE

To my mind this is the most importance stance. In my main style of karate (Japanese Gen Sei Ryu) it is **the** critical stance. Bring either your right or left foot back to a position perpendicular with your front foot. The distance between your front and rear foot is about one and one-half times the width of your shoulders. The heels of your front and rear feet are in a straight line. Your front toes should be facing forward and your rear toes to the right. Your feet are flat on the floor with your rear leg, hips and body in an almost vertical line. Both of your knees are bent, and seventy percent of your body weight is supported by your back leg. Your front knee is pressed forward to push your body weight towards your rear leg. Your front foot extends further from your body than your leg.

Extremely important, your upper body should be straight no matter what type of posture you are in. If you are going to be off balance in any stance, lean backward rather than forward. You can easily move forward or backward in this stance, because both of your legs are already bent. Remember to keep most of your weight on your back leg. When stepping forward first shift your body weight from your front foot and push your body forward with your rear foot. Reverse the procedure when stepping backward.

Be careful in changing stances and alert to your opponent's changes in stance. Visualize two individuals in combat. The attacker is at Point A, and the defender at Point B. The attacker moves from Point A towards Point B and changes stance from one side to the other while going forward. If the defender nails the attacker in the middle of their stance change, the attacker will be caught off balance and unprotected, and should be scored upon easily. Look for any opening your opponent gives you. React to what they do rather than following any prearranged battle plan of your own.

In the back stance you can pivot on the heel of your back foot or lift up your front foot. By pushing against the floor and stepping you can pivot 360 degrees and let your opponent tire themselves out trying to get behind you!

HORSEBACK RIDING STANCE

The horseback riding stance is a strong well-balanced posture, but does have a deficiency of mobility. Your feet should be spread to the side parallel to each other at a distance twice your natural standing width. Pretending you are mounted on a horse, bend your knees outward and sink your rear end down. Your hips should be pushed to the rear with your upper body straight and centered in the middle of both legs. Your upper body including your legs should be taut and your upper body relaxed.

SIDE STANCE

The side stance is basically similar to the horseback riding stance except that it is executed when your opponent is at your side. You attack your opponent by bringing your right foot over your left or moving in a straight line to the side and pushing out to the left. To retreat you simply reverse the procedure.

FORWARD STANCE

The forward stance is of extremely limited value in a street fight. This stance leaves too many openings to defend. Your front toes point straight forward, your front knee bent. Your back knee is straight with the toes of your back foot at approximately a 30 degree angle to the right. Your body weight should be distributed with sixty percent on the front foot. Your upper body is held straight in a front-facing posture. To move forward you bring your rear leg to the front until your rear foot is at about a 30 degree angle with your knee slightly bent. Reverse the procedure for going backward.

CAT STANCE

The cat stance is extremely mobile and good for fast shifting. There is little distance between your feet which are almost touching with one slightly in front of the other. Your body weight rests principally on your rear foot which is flat on the floor with your knee slightly bent. The ball of the front foot simply touches the floor. Your rear knee should be tensed inward. Your front leg should be easily lifted from the floor for a kick without shifting your body weight.

ON-THE-FLOOR POSITION

The very idea of fighting from the floor is rather upsetting to most Americans, especially males, who have been raised on the old shibboleth of staying on one's feet no matter what. Orientals have never had this sort of ego problem! American devotees of the Asiatic fighting arts have long been aware of these techniques. The whole world watched them in action when Muhammad Ali fought a Japanese wrestler in Tokyo. A lot of Americans thought the Japanese grappler's techniques were ludicrous, because he stayed in a prone position for most of the fight. Completely overlooked was the fact that the gentleman from Japan got a draw with the Heavyweight Champion of the World!

After the bout it was Ali who was obliged to seek medical attention, not the uninjured wrestler! So much for the disadvantages of fighting from the ground.

The best way to get into position for on-the-ground fighting is from a back stance. Drop to the ground in a side position and using your hip as a fulcrum pivot on it. Mobility along the ground is aided by your bottom elbow which is pushed against the floor. Your top foot is extended far enough to the front so that your groin area is covered from a standing opponent's kick. It is pushed against the floor lifted up and put down again to help you in your progress along the ground. From this position you can throw the side kick, front kick, roundhouse kick, or practically any kick that you can unleash when standing. And using your legs as a pair of scissors you can catch your opponent's leg in a two-way pincer movement.

When fighting a foe who is using this technique, if your leg is caught in the scissors movement hold the trapped leg straight and you will not fall.

This on-the-floor technique works best for the lighter, more agile fighter. A heavyset individual should not attempt it except when absolutely necessary.

There are many minor variations of these basic stances, but explaining them in fine detail would be beyond the intention of this book.

CHAPTER FIVE

THE VITAL HAND BLOWS

As if he were a ballet dancer the fighter lashed out at his opponent with kick after roundhouse kick. He was all feet until he suddenly ducked under his opponent's guard and attacked with lefts and rights to both sides of the neck. Again and again he pounded the area while the other, completely helpless, stood there dazed and then collapsed. It took over five minutes to revive him.

The woman cowered against a wall. The man pressed his palm against the side of her neck. She gave a gasp. Her bladder and bowels emptied themselves of their contents after her heart stopped beating, and she fell lifeless to the floor.

Dr. Yoshiaki, M.D., Sc.D. is an outstanding authority in Oriental medicine. He is Director of Medical Research of the Heart Disease

Foundation in New York City, and Visiting Research Professor of Electrical Engineering at Manhattan College. I asked him: What happens when a blow hits the carotid artery/vagus nerve area?" He said the heart can stop momentarily. In the case of someone with heart trouble, the heart may not start working again. If the victim is afflicted with high blood pressure a stroke might result from the rupturing of a blood vessel because the blood pressure is suddenly raised and lowered quickly. This causes dizziness and complete mental confusion for a period of five to twenty seconds. The person is helpless and therefore it is easy for anyone, even the proverbial little old lady, to inflict any form of physical punishment on even the greatest champion without him or her being able to resist.

The carotid artery and vagus nerve area is located on both sides of the neck. The artery's pulsations can be easily felt by placing one's finger on the vessel just above the collarbone. The point here is that it is not so much the type of blow as where it hits that counts. Of course many types of strikes can be applied to a vulnerable area.

THE SLAP

Most Americans consider the slap a blow from a coy maiden trying to ward off the advances of an ardent suitor. But the slap can be a most potent weapon when properly applied. The trick here is to slap with a cupped open hand. If you slap with stretched fingers you cover more surface but you lose concentration, and more important you lose the power transmitted through the cupped enclosure. Force is accentuated by bringing your power from the turn of the wrist rather than from the arm alone.

When you slap the air is compacted by the force exerted and the power effect is multiplied. It is important to keep the thumb closely glued to the index finger. The facial nerves of even an experienced boxer cannot withstand this effect. Your aim is to act upon the facial nerves. The pain induced is intense. The force penetrates deep inside the head to a central knot of facial nerves called "Ganglion Gasseri". This knot is headquarters for the nerves of sensation that serve the eyes, the upper jaw, and the lower jaw. When the knot is disturbed by a cupped-slap, real havoc is caused. You can't focus your eyes, your orientation sense goes awry, and often you lose consciousness. The last is something of a blessing, because the pain of "tic douloureux" (trigeminal neuralgia) is called by many physicians the worst pain a human being can endure!

THE REVERSE PUNCH

The karate reverse punch is one of the most potent of all unarmed self-defense weapons. In order to be able to throw this awful missile of destruction one must first learn to make the proper karate fist.

Your palm should be facing outward, the fingers bent slightly at the first joint. The fingers are folded over again into the palm. Tuck the thumb underneath the fist. Only the first two knuckles should come into contact with the target. The front of the hand should be flat and square. The wrist should be straight or only slightly bent. A bent wrist is apt to be a broken wrist when throwing this type of blow.

In executing this type of punch one must keep in mind that the shortest distance between two points is a straight line. One must also be relaxed until point of contact. Tense at that moment and then relax as your hand returns to its starting position at your waist. When your fist leaves your side in a straight line to the target your palm is up. Just before point of contact the palm is turned down. Inhale during your fist's movement to the target, and exhale at the point of contact.

If this seems like a lot to remember, it is. But practice makes perfect. A hundred repetitions per day for a six month period will make the move a reflex action. Remember, if you have to think about what you are going to do in a fight you've already lost. **If you have time to practice only one blow, let this be the one**

THE BACK FIST

The back fist is a punch that completely bewilders those who do not have any Oriental fighting arts training. With your right palm facing forward, cock your fist behind your left shoulder blade. You deliver the punch in a vertical arc. As in the reverse punch the two knuckles are all that should come in contact with your target. The blow should be delivered with one snapping motion of the arm. The elbow should be bent otherwise the joint may be injured. There are three ways to throw this blow: downward, outward, and curving upward. Your targets are the head, face, temple, chin, chest, solar plexus, ribs, kidneys and back.

THE PALM HEEL

Its name adequately describes this strike. It is a blow with the heel of the palm. For a right-hand palm heel strike, cock the heel of your palm at your right wrist. Thrust it forward with the palm facing forward and the outer edge of the hand pointing downward. When attacking a high target you twist your arm inwards so that the outer edge of your hand faces to the right. Possible target areas are the head, face, nose temple, chin, solar plexus, rib cage, floating ribs and kidneys. There are four basic ways to deliver this blow: forward, upward, downward, and hooking.

THE SPEAR HAND

To remake your hand into something resembling a spear point hold your fingers tightly together, the three middle finger tips even in height. Thrust in a straight line at the solar plexus, eyes, throat, floating ribs or kidneys when throwing a spear hand.

THE UPPERCUT

An uppercut is a strike featuring the fore-fist in an upward arc without the arms being fully extended. The elbow is bent and held close to the body. Best areas to hit are the chin, solar plexus, ribs and kidneys.

THE HOOK PUNCH

The hook punch is delivered in a narrow horizontal arc, striking with the fore-fist without the full extension of the arms. This close-range blow's power comes from the body, as in the uppercut punch. The best targets are the face, chin, solar plexus, ribs and kidneys.

THE HAMMER FIST

The bottom of the fist is utilized in the hammer fist, usually striking in a downward arc. This blow is particularly effective against the head, temple, collarbone, and base of the neck.

THE JUDO PUNCH

The judo punch is a strike in which the knuckles are formed in different orientations. It is most effective against weak areas such as eyes, temple, throat, bridge of the nose and kidneys.

THE RIDGE HAND

The **inner** edge of the hand is utilized in a horizontal arc when employing the ridge hand. It is particularly effective against vulnerable areas such as the eyes, bridge of the nose, chin, temple and throat.

THE BACK HAND

The back of the hand is utilized primarily in an outward direction when throwing a back hand strike. Although it is an extremely weak blow it can nevertheless be used as a block to deflect an attacking hand. The most likely targets are the ears, eyes and groin.

Remember, as described in the REVERSE PUNCH above, the formation of the **"karate fist"** is critical, and applies to each of the above strikes.

CHAPTER SIX
GET YOUR KICKS

Here is a potpourri of techniques that, if practiced thoroughly and executed successfully, ought to make you the victor in any melee. Locate some suitable sparring partners and practice, practice, practice!

FRONT KICK

In a street fight, the front snap kick is the most useful of all leg maneuvers. **If you have time to practice only one kick, let this be the one.** It is perfect for combinations of hand and foot attacks because you can easily maintain balance after kicking. Raise your knee so that the upper leg is parallel with the floor. The lower leg should be cocked backwards, towards the thigh. There is a snapping motion of your knee when throwing the kick. The thigh is raised slightly. The foot is then brought back to the cocked position and lowered to the floor. The delivery and return of the foot to the cocked position must be executed in one continuous snapping motion. This prevents your enemy from catching your foot and breaking it and puts you in position for the next kick. Your targets are practically any place on the middle or upper body.

KNEE KICK

The most lethal kick is the knee kick. There are two types, front and roundhouse. The front knee kick is delivered straightforward, while the roundhouse knee kick is delivered in a circular motion from side to front. For the front knee kick raise the knee into an uppercut position. For the right roundhouse knee kick, go into a forward stance. Cock the kicking leg on your side with the lower leg bent slightly back against the thigh and the upper leg parallel to the floor and extended almost to your right side. Deliver the kick in a circular motion by pivoting the supporting foot and swinging the hips slightly to the left while twisting your body to the right to maintain balance. The most likely targets for either knee kick are your opponent's groin, or his head after you have brought it downward with your hands.

SIDE KICK

The side thrust kick can be aimed at high, middle or low targets. Assume a side stance and step with your right foot over and behind your left. Bend your left knee, bringing the left leg up on your left side with the foot close to the supporting knee. Then raise the kicking foot, attempting to face it directly to the target. Simultaneously extend it straight out to the side almost parallel to the floor with the full power of your hip and upper body. Make sure to put your hip into it. Then pull your leg back to the cocked position and return to the side stance.

STAMPING KICK (HEEL AND SIDE EDGE)

An unspectacular looking but extremely devastating blow is the stamping kick. Go into the forward stance, and cock the rear foot by raising the knee close to the chest. For a heel kick, the ankle must be flexed upward with the heel down, enabling you to thrust to the front, back or sides of your foe's legs. For a side edge stamping kick your leg is cocked as in the side kick. Return it instantly to its cocked position after firing it off and then put it on the floor.

ANKLE KICK

One of the most effective kicks for an on-the-street encounter is the ankle kick. Its primary target is the enemy's knee in the front, back or sides. Throw this blow the same as the side kick by first raising the kicking foot to the height of the knee of the enemy's supporting leg. Then, combining a snap with your kicking leg and a spring in your supporting one, let fly! <u>It only takes three pounds of pressure to demolish your enemy's knee</u>. If you are unshod keep the big toe bent back and the heel jutting out of your kicking leg.

ROUNDHOUSE KICK

When I refer here to the roundhouse kick I mean a **front** roundhouse kick. The full roundhouse kick takes too long to throw to be really effective in a street fight. This kick is performed from a back stance. Cock your front leg slightly, pressing your kicking knee inward and the foot outward, placing it off to your side in front of your hip. Then send the kick to its target by raising the leg and kicking sharply inward as the leg is about to connect with your opponent.

The target areas are the middle and upper parts of the body.

CRESCENT KICK (REGULAR AND OUTER-EDGE)

The crescent kick is made by cocking your leg in a manner somewhat similar to the front kick except that it is held in an oblique direction between your front and right side. Open the knee in order to be able to raise the kicking foot. Deliver the kick in a circular motion to your left, by swinging your hips while twisting your body. The kicking leg must be in front of your body.

The outer-edge crescent kick is delivered in the opposite direction from that of the regular crescent kick. The outer edge of the foot is the striking surface. The inner-edge crescent kick has as its striking surface the inner edge of the foot. This kick is a good weapon to deflect your foe's hand or to hit the temple.

FOOT SWEEP

For the foot sweep, the inverted arch of your foot should be aimed at the instep of your opponent. If you execute it correctly he should be literally swept off his feet!

Once again, the only road to proficiency is practice, practice and more practice.

CHAPTER SEVEN

BLOCK, DEFEND, WIN

Blocking is the hardest part of pugilistic training to teach a beginning student. Moreover, we must emphasize that in full-contact karate many of the traditional blocks are of little practical value.

As with the punch and the kick, the block is most effective if you put all your strength into the blocking hand at the instant of contact. As in other strikes, relax your body until point of contact.

UPPER BLOCK

For the upper block bring your hand with the top down to below the armpit on the opposite side of your body. With the lower arm parallel to the ground move it upward in an arc. Block upward on a diagonal as you turn your arm outward.

MIDDLE INSIDE BLOCK

The middle inside block is performed in the same manner as the upper block except that your blocking hand is at the middle of your body.

FORE-FIST MIDDLE OUTSIDE (INSIDE) BLOCK

For the fore-fist middle outside block bring your hand up behind your ear on the same side. Then turn your arm inward and swing it outward (INSIDE) in a semicircle, and down.

INSIDE BLOCK AND LOW PARRY

With your hand cocked at your side bring your other hand to the middle of your chest and cross it at the wrist with your withdrawn hand. Raise your hand to near your ear on the opposite side. Then bring your hand down, going to the outside as you block. Now combine the inside block and the low parry for a very effective block. Cross your arms at your side, and be sure to put your blocking hand on top.

KNIFE HAND UPPER BLOCK

In a knife hand block the fleshy part of your hand should come in contact with your target. The knife hand upper block starts from behind your ear with your hand in a cupping position. Then your hand turns in a semicircle and outward to block.

KNIFE HAND MIDDLE INSIDE BLOCK

This block is performed the same as the fore-fist middle inside block except that the hand position is a knife hand.

PALM HEEL UPPER BLOCK

The palm heel upper block is performed by shooting out your palm heel from the side position with your palm down. When you strike a target your palm is up. This is a situation for light blocking techniques. It deflects or guides your opponent's blows away from you using less strength than he.

PALM HEEL MIDDLE OUTSIDE BLOCK

In this block you throw your palm heel from the middle of your body.

PALM HEEL LOWER BLOCK

This block is performed the same way as the others except that you block downward.

WRIST MIDDLE OUTSIDE BLOCK

This block is similar to the above except that you block with your wrist.

CHINESE WATER WHEEL

This is my favorite block! It is light blocking at its ultimate. One hand is held high over your head, with your other hand held below your groin. Your hands can be in either an open palm position or in a closed fist position. Your hands go forward, with one hand rising as the other descends.

KATA

Kata are prearranged fighting moves performed in sequence. Performing kata is a good way to practice the above moves. Many American martial arts instructors decry the teaching of kata as having no practical value for learning fighting techniques. With all due respect to my colleagues, I disagree. Of course the performance of kata cannot be considered a substitute for a sparring session with a live partner, nevertheless, it is the next best thing to it.

FOUR WAY BLOCK AND PUNCH KATA

This kata contains all the basic moves necessary for a successful defense. After bowing (one must respect the traditions) perform five sequential moves. They are the same five moves for each of eight positions; the ninth and last position is a variant.   Standing in a left-side back-stance, block with a back hand, throw two punches (right and left) and then a front kick. Punch with your right hand, lift up the front part of your feet, and pivot on your heels 180 degrees. When you are in this position number two, repeat the procedure and then go to position number three. To get there, bring your lead foot back with your heel hitting the heel of your other foot. Your lead foot becomes your rear foot as your position is changed 90 degrees to the left.

Repeat the five moves and then go to position number four by pivoting on your heels 180 degrees. Repeat the drill. To go to position number five bring your lead foot back as you did in changing from position two to position three. All of these position moves are identical, except for position number nine where you step forward, change from the back stance to the front stance, and throw left and right reverse punches. You then bow once more, and the kata is over.

Even if you have no one with whom you can practice that is no excuse for not working out. You can study and repeat the kata to master your self-defense moves.

There are a variety of practical defenses that are easy to learn and to apply in a confrontation.

WRIST GRAB

To defend yourself when your wrist is grabbed turn your free hand in, palm towards your body. Take hold of your opponents are at the wrist, pressing up as you press down with your held arm. As your arm is released you place your free hand under his elbow locking it, and press up on his elbow while twisting his wrist outward.

HANDSHAKE

A handshake isn't always a sign of friendship. It can be the beginning of an attack. If this should happen to you step in and place your left hand over his right, pressing his thumb down and back. Continue the pressure on his thumb even after he releases your hand, and step back. Then, still maintaining the pressure on the thumb, drop to one knee, twist his wrist to the left and throw him.

COLLAR GRAB

Your assailant comes up behind you and grabs you by the back of the collar. Drop to your left knee and move under his arm. Place your left arm between his legs from behind and lift his leg off the ground. Switch arms so you can bring pressure to his chest and bring him to the ground.

MIDSECTION ATTACK

Your assailant moves in on you with an attack to your midsection. Sidestep and block the punch with a downward strike of your left hand. Grab his wrist with your blocking hand and bring your other hand underneath to cup his hand. Step in while applying downward pressure with your fingers and pressing on the back of his hands with your thumbs. Drop to one knee and twist his arm to the outside while continuing the pressure, then throw him.

THE CHOKE

A mugger tries to choke you. Throw a quick punch to the attacker's face. Note that the double punch makes contact inside the choke hold so that your arms serve also as an effective block. Taking a step backwards and grabbing both of the attacker's arms pull the opponent in to you and throw a snap front kick to the solar plexus. Proceed to twist and spin the attacker at will!

THE GROIN ATTACK

An attacker throws a kick at your groin. The kick can be stopped in mid-air with a straight forward punch to the shin bone. This blow requires precise focus and a good deal of strength. Straighten up and follow through with a right straight forward punch to the attacker's chin. Use a swiveling hip movement to support and reinforce the force of your blow. This is followed up with a roundhouse kick to the lower rib cage, which in turn is followed up by a spinning of the attacker and a take down.

For another defense of a groin kick, block the blow with the broad side of your leg. Follow through with force pushing the attacker's kick away. Plant your right foot behind him, then step in quickly and grab the attacker's clothing at the waist and sweep his body backward over that right foot. The action is completed with a kick to any part of the attacker's body.

THE FACE PUNCH

An attacker throws a punch at your face. Elude the blow by ducking under it. At the same time raise your left hand palm out as a stop-block, just in case the attacker's arm should move down and in. The block is made with an open palm so that it can protect the surface of your face. At the same time strike at the attacker's exposed throat with fingers knuckled at the second joint.

An attacker fancies himself as a boxer and throws a jab at your face. You block the blow with a palm-heel to the outside of the attacker's forearm, which pushes him off balance. Grab him by the coat sleeve and at the same time cock your foot and throw a side kick to the lower rib cage area. You then spin your foe sweeping him to the ground with your right foot.

An attacker standing in front of you throws a punch. You block it with a hard forearm block, thrown as hard as possible. The objective is to break the arm throwing the punch. Then grab the opponent's wrist or sleeve, and pivoting swing the opponent in a quarter-circle. Follow through with a right-hand blow to the solar plexus and lower rib cage area. The circle-swing is to disorient the attacker to set him up for the follow through. Your coup de grace is a shuto (chop) to the back of the attacker's neck. This entire sequence, block, swing, punch and chop should be performed in one continuous movement.

The following situations will serve to illustrate the use of blocks in a variety of street confrontation scenarios:

In a common street situation when your opponent throws a roundhouse punch, stop it with an open-hand overhand block. Retaliate with a ridge hand strike to the head while grabbing his punching arm at the wrist with your blocking hand. Follow with a hand and hip throw. Prevent him from retaliating by locking his wrist.

You block a thug's punch with an open hand. While holding on to the thief's punching arm, extend the block into a punch to the upper ribs. Lift the thief's arm above his head holding his arm in a clenched fist. Bring his arm down and away from his body, readying for a punch. Drive a punch into his ribs. Then grab him by the shoulder and bring his head to your raised knee. Follow up with a punch to the groin and a shuto (chop) to his neck. Finish by driving a kick into the back of his knee, holding him to the ground with your right hand gripping his left shoulder.

A man tries to hit you with a club. You sidestep the initial blow. Block and snap a front kick into the attacker's stomach. Then employ a joint-locking technique to immobilize and control the attacker's arm. Apply leverage to render him helpless.

A front kick by your opponent is blocked and deflected by your forward arm. Holding on to his leg by the ankle with your blocking arm you deliver a reverse punch to the head. Releasing your hold on the ankle and catching and pressing up and forward on his knee with your bicep will easily drop him on the ground where strikes can finish him.

As a snap side kick is delivered by your opponent, your leading hand blocks it to the side. The arm closest to your body holds the leg, lifting it and breaking his balance at the same time. Your leading hand now becomes the striking hand.

An opponent makes a grab for your throat. You counter with an inside double hand block. Grab the opponent by the wrists and spread his arms apart. Twist inward and cross his arms, and throw him by twisting his wrists and pulling him forward and over. On the ground, prevent him from recovering by holding his arms crossed and applying strong pressure to his right wrist.

An attacker charges forward with a roundhouse or thrust punch. You move back and block with a ridge hand block. Drop back on your left foot, grab his collar and twist it under his jaw while pulling him forward. Then drop to one knee and bring him over and to the ground. Retaining hold of his collar and arm use an arm bar with bladed hand across his throat. Twist the arm and push to cut off air to his windpipe.

When approached on the street by an attacker swinging a club, your first reaction should be to block the weapon. Then deliver a strike or pressure-grab aimed at the windpipe (a highly sensitive area) which should temporarily put the attacker out of commission. Then use a palm-heel strike to the solar plexus to bring him to his knees, finishing with a knee to the chin or face.

An assailant throws a straight punch to your chest. You block with your left arm and immediately grab his arm at the wrist with your right hand. Throw a back fist to his face, a shuto to his throat, and then sweep him to the ground and deliver a finishing kick to the face.

You side-step a kick, blocking it sharply with an upsweep of your right arm. The same arm delivers a back fist to your foe's head. Grab him by the back of his head with your left hand, bringing his head down into your rising knee. A sharp right arm to the throat quickly turns into a disabling headlock.

You are confronted by two attackers. As one of them throws a roundhouse kick at your groin you use a leg block to neutralize the blow. Quickly stepping forward grab the man's arm and prepare for your counterattack. Twisting your body smash your arm into the back of the man's head, followed instantly by a knee kick to his face. As the second thug throws a punch, deflect his blow and ready your offense. Smash a side kick into the man's ribs, and execute a front leg sweep to send the thug sprawling. Finish with appropriate kicks and blows.

A karate-trained mugger attacks you. From a fighting stance the attacker is set for a roundhouse kick. You stop this with a forearm block, sweep his front leg, and affect a takedown from this position.

You and a mugger square off with you using a waterwheel block. He moves in and throws a punch. You catch his arm in a two-handed pressure hold, and by exerting pressure on his elbow you force him to the floor.

When your opponent throws a straight punch at your chest you stop it with a middle block. Grab his right sleeve at the wrist. Then bring your leg up and throw a reverse crescent kick to his elbow and a side kick to his rib cage. All during this sequence you retain hold of his jacket so that he cannot move out of reach.

<u>Soft blocks followed by hard counters are the ultimate in karate techniques.</u> Here are a few sequences you can employ:

Using a hook block, your forward arm catches and deflects a punch, forcing an opponent's arm to the outside and leaving his side open to attack.

Beginning with a hook block to the outside you grab the striking arm at the wrist and deliver a sharp punch to the attacker's side.Raise his striking arm up and over your body and grasp the same with your opposite arm to free your forward hand so that you can deliver a back-fist to his face.

As an opponent moves in with a punch you can employ the combination block. Your rear arm deflects the punch as your forward arm rises to continue to push your opponent to the outside. This releases your rear arm for your counterattack.

A variation of the combination block is to push the attacking arm up and out, rather than just to the outside. This leaves him wide open for a punch to the armpit.

Only through practice and repetition of these blocks and defenses will you become sufficiently proficient to protect yourself in these all-to-common street confrontations. You must practice with a friend, carefully going through the techniques in slow motion. To become truly proficient your actions must become reflex.

The ability to block an opponent's blow and retaliate instantly is the sure-fire formula for success in any street encounter. To mix the ingredients successfully one must make the transition from blocking to throwing a blow smoothly with no mental hesitation.

All the moves must flow naturally from one to the other. Often the only difference between the winner and the loser of a fight is the absence of indecision on the winner's part. Constant practice of techniques without counting each step mentally will help to achieve the desired results.

CHAPTER EIGHT

THE BRAIN DEFENSE

"Hey, you son of a bitch!" The outdoor dinner guests started at the intrusion of four men and a woman. With a roguish gleam in her eyes the woman looked directly at a portly man and repeated her obscenity. Momentarily taken aback the gentleman nevertheless regained his composure and redirected his attention to his dinner companion. Enraged, the drunken woman stumbled slightly and then lunged for the nearest dinner knife. With a circular motion she made a superficial cut around his throat. Ashen faced, the man recoiled in disbelief as blood began to flow from the wound. His female companion shrieked at the assailant: "Why you crazy bitch! Look what you've done." The intoxicated woman answered with a wild slap high on the other woman's cheek.

At this point the host attempted to evict the intruders, but the drunken woman made a thrusting motion at him with her fingers. He blocked her blow and slapped the woman's face. Blinding pain then tore into the host as he was rabbit-punched to the floor by one of the woman's male companions. A shoe smashed his nose, and blood erupted like a geyser.

The above vignette is from a letter written to one of the country's leading karate magazines. It continues in the writer's own words: "I regained my feet and prepared to defend myself as well as possible even though injured (my nose was broken) and outnumbered."

"In the days that followed this incident people invariably asked me: 'Why didn't you use your karate?' My reply follows: Karate does not make anyone invincible, despite what you may see in movies or read in 10-easy-lessons ads.

Karate **does** prepare you to react calmly and prudently under normal as well as adverse circumstances. Karate accomplishes this through mental as well as physical training. Karate instills in the student an excellent moral code along with the physical aspects of self-defense training. Master Gichin Funakoshi said: 'A truly great man is not disturbed even when confronted with an unexpected event or crisis, nor angered upon finding himself in situations not of his own making.'

When this incident took place most of my friends were either hysterical or on the verge of hysteria. They were not prepared to handle an emergency situation. I was, through the moral and spiritual discipline of karate. Even though the situation looked grim I did not panic. I was not scared. I was ready, willing and able to defend myself if necessary. I smiled and apologized to my friends for the rude interruption in an otherwise wonderful evening. I asked the party crashers if they could explain why they had brought unhappiness and violence to my home. They left without answering or causing any further disturbances.

To me, this was true karate in action. I was able to gain control of the situation without resorting to heedless and foolish violence. I was proud of the way I handled the problem and I am even prouder now. Master Funakoshi said: 'Force is used as a last resort where humanity and justice cannot prevail.' "

Most people think karate consists of physical violence, breaking boards and bricks. Everyone seems to know a Black Belt who is a deadly killer. There is, however, a mental side to karate that is **far more useful.** It is this mental and spiritual side of karate that I have been trying to depict by including this letter.

Hopefully it has provided an adequate illustration.

Recalling his fight-a-night routine with hecklers in the days before he studied karate, Buddy Rich said: "You find it unbelievable?" He called to a member of his staff: "Hey, tell him about the fights!"

And after his aide verified the stories, the world's greatest drummer laughed, the glow from his pearly white teeth illuminating the corner of the dark ballroom where we sat.

"Just because someone mouths off at me, I don't start to fight unless someone actually lays his hands on me. I suppose it's because I now feel reassured about my own fighting ability. I don't have to prove myself any longer. Karate has brought me peace of mind. In fact I feel karate is my life now. I feel it holds a much more important place in my existence than my music, and what I want to do is quit being a performer for a year and go over to Japan and just study karate!"

When asked whether karate has changed other people's outlook towards him, Rich said: "When I used to give concerts at the different college campuses, a small minority of the kids used to be a little rough on me. After a few articles came out about me playing karate I was treated very respectfully. After I demonstrated karate with my teacher Aaron Banks on the Dick Cavett Show the respect was even more pronounced! That doesn't mean I want anybody to call me 'Sir' or even 'Mr. Rich'. I'm 'Buddy' to everyone, whether he's the president of the United States or a porter. What I mean is I don't want to have any hassles." I believe most of us would say "Amen" to those sentiments.

The power of the mind is beyond understanding. The reader will undoubtedly think the following is a rather gory fairy tale: "The knife took on a life of its own, and the man scarcely noticed the youth holding it. His left hand reached out, and grasping the knife by the blade he turned it into the young thug's body. At the same time his right fist shot out, the hand opened, and the tensed fingers jabbed into the attacker's eyes."

Now surely no one in the world can grab a knife by the blade without being cut, certainly not the untrained reader of this book. Yet it may surprise you to know that several years ago I had a class of fourth grade girls who learned this technique in one lesson, to the amazement of their parents!

In one of my own exhibitions a student attempted to attack me with a razor-sharp machete. I caught the weapon by the blade with one hand and twisted it out of the student's control, while my other hand attacked his eyes and Adam's apple. As a finale, I crushed double-edged razor blades in my palms. My secret was **mind power.** I simply willed my skin not to bleed.

I first learned about this technique when I read Mastau Oyama's classic *This Is Karate.* According to Oyama: "When grasping a knife by the blade if you firmly take hold of the blade with confidence that it will not cut you, it will not cut you." I admit that when I first read that passage I was skeptical. However, after I had learned more of this karate philosophy it became one of the techniques I used in my exhibitions. It is the most effective way to save your life when threatened by someone with a knife.

Despite all you may have seen and read about kicking a weapon out of somebody's hand, it is not a practical idea. The person with the weapon has all the advantages. If pitted against most of the Black Belts in the martial arts (one at a time) he could easily kill or wound them.

As for the usual kick-the-knife-out-of-the-opponent's-hand routine, I recall a time in my younger days when I was a Purple Belt. I let a fellow karateka kick my hand 500 times to see if I would be forced to open my hand and drop a wooden knife. I never dropped the knife, though for the next few weeks my hand was swollen and black and blue! So much for useless techniques.

When you grab a knife by the blade you must believe you will not be cut. If your opponent attempts to pull the knife backwards or lunges forward, go along with the movement. Whichever way he goes with the blade go along with it. As long as your hand is wrapped around the weapon you should be able to keep from being stabbed. Of course the ideal fighting condition is to turn the knife back into the enemy. **Even better, run like hell if you can.** This technique is only for when there is no way out.

There are times, however, when your opponent's mind power can work against you. For example, the question often arises as to whether it is easier to fight an addict or an unhooked person. In a way it is easier to fight a junkie because he is the leading character in his own slow-motion movie. On the other hand, the narcotics-user may be so filled with pain-relieving drugs that if a sledgehammer hit him he would scarcely feel it.

Mind power can work against you in another way. Your opponent may have a real taste for violence while you are by nature peaceful. As pointed out in Chapter Three, it is important not to hesitate, and to <u>never rely on one blow to do the job.</u> Strike with everything you have. Throw anything you can lay your hands on including the "kitchen sink" into the fray in a strong barrage. Remember, even if you deal your opponent a fatal blow if he is able to return the courtesy before succumbing you're both losers.

Never forget that the average hoodlum has a lot of street-fighting experience. He is usually a determined fighter and won't follow the Marquis of Queensbury rules. To win over this attacker you have to fight dirty ….. <u>dirtier than he does.</u> When you are fighting for your life you are not playing games.

Sensei Pete Siringano likes to tell the story of a prospective student who was amazed at the flawless techniques of another student. He asked: "Sensei, how do you think this Black Belt would do in a street situation?" Siringano said flatly: "He would be slaughtered <u>because he doesn't want to kill.</u>"

An instructor once said to me: "I always ask my Black Belts 'Are you willing to kill if you have to?' If they say no, then I say that their martial arts education is wasted, except as a form of healthful exercise." <u>If you are seriously interested in self-defense you have to be ready to kill.</u> Your mental attitude toward facing a dangerous confrontation is every bit as important as your skill.

Master Yoshiteru Otani tells a story of a famous Japanese samurai who was walking along a road and met an equally well-known Master of the Tea Ceremony. The samurai challenged the other to a duel. The Tea Master said: "I have an appointment. I will meet you here in two hours." Then he ran off to a fencing school and begged the instructor: "Teach me how to use the sword." The instructor assured him there was no way to learn the weapon's use in two hours and asked: "Are you willing to die?"

"Yes", replied the Tea Master. "I too am descended from warriors."

Said the instructor: "As he starts to cut your body in half with a side slice (a well-known common technique) bring down your sword and chop his head in half." Armed with this advice and a borrowed sword the Tea Master returned on time for the confrontation. When the samurai saw him poised for the head chop, and realizing he too would die, he said: "This is foolish. Why don't we call off the duel? And teach me the Tea Ceremony instead." It is reported that they both expired peacefully in their beds many years later.

Remember, the criminal doesn't want to die any more than you do. A brave determined front **can** save your life. But it can't be only a front. You have to be ready to follow through. This mental attitude is a critical part of the martial arts philosophy. Keep in mind, however, that this is not a clarion call for "hotheads" to flare up at the slightest provocation.

Never forget that <u>expertise is not insurance</u>. No amount of training or protection, including bodyguards, can insure absolute safety for anyone. No human being by reason of his mortality can expect complete immunity from harm. Yet the overwhelming majority of people go into karate (self-defense) with this fairy-tale concept of security in mind.

The writer of the letter at the beginning of this chapter used his most important weapon in his battle for survival......<u>his head!</u>   The heroic response to impress his guests would have been to retaliate in kind and in all likelihood cause some of his friends to be injured in the ensuing melee and perhaps get himself killed as well. Instead he used his head and talked his way out of trouble.

CHAPTER NINE

<u>THE FOURTEEN KEY RULES</u>

I hope I've made the point throughout this book that the techniques shown in entertainment-land are simply not authentic. There are many false notions about fighting that the movie and television industries have created. Because the process of "unlearning" is harder than learning you must rid yourself of those false notions. Below are my fourteen rules of what **<u>not</u>** to do in a street brawl.

<u>RULE NUMBER ONE</u>

Do not get into a street confrontation unless it is unavoidable. Run, don't walk, away from such an incident. No matter how innocent you are convinced you are, for an exorbitant fee any lawyer will tell you that your guilt or innocence may have no bearing on the outcome of your court case.

RULE NUMBER TWO

If you do get into a fight, whatever the reason, you must never use more strength than your opponent is using against you. This may sound silly, and it is, nevertheless it's the law, like it or not. For more about self-defense and the law see Chapter Eighteen.

RULE NUMBER THREE

Remember, you're nor Superman or Superwoman. As Sensei Yoshiteru Otani, the highest ranking all-around martial artist in the world said: "I know much more about fighting than the average man, but that does not mean I go into a telephone booth as mild-mannered businessman Yoshiteru Otani and emerge as Superman Otani simply because I hold all of these high martial arts degrees. As any Black Belt knows, against one person the Black Belt may emerge the victor. Against many he may be as helpless as a little old lady. That is why in the U. S. Budo Federation we stress the character-building and exercise effects instead of Superman comic book feats."

Sensei Otani feels this is one of the reasons for the enormous drop-out rate in the American fighting arts. In the nation as a whole over 98% of martial arts students quit before attaining Black Belt rank. Most martial arts advertising implies that the student will become a master killer in ten easy lessons. In reality the student is still an easy target for any street-wise thug.

He told me a story that illustrates his concept of what the average American thinks of the martial artist's capabilities and how they really should be used. A Japanese folk tale tells of a horse noted for its extraordinary kicking ability. The animal stood guard at the beginning of a road. A Kendo Master and his disciple wished to travel this road, but the horse straddled the path and blocked their way. The Master said: "I will try to avoid getting kicked", and passed in front of the horse without incident. The disciple puffed up his chest and declared: "I am not afraid of **any** horse." He went around the rear of the horse and was immediately kicked unconscious for his foolishness! Sensei Otani smiled and said: "I, like the ancient Master, will always try to **avoid** getting into trouble."

RULE NUMBER FOUR

If your opponent has a weapon, do not try to use hand and foot techniques. Get yourself a weapon too. False heroics are strictly for movies and television. I asked one instructor if he thought his karate capabilities would protect him from a street mugger. A Yodan, he replied: "Hell no, if what you mean by karate is strictly hands and feet!" To Orientals weapons have a definite place in karate. In Japan students are instructed in their use at the very beginning level.

When asked if some of his methods might be illegal he replied: "What's legal about somebody trying to take my life, or the life of a member of my family? In a street mugging an addict doesn't give a damn if you're a Black Belt. All he knows is that he is going to kill or maim you for life so he can get money for another fix. In a situation like that it is either kill or be killed. If a person has a weapon he should use it on the attacker. The only rule is **do it first!**"

Another martial arts Master, Daniel K. Pai, agrees. In one workout session Master Pai tossed about twenty knives onto the floor and told each student to pick one up. "How would you fight with a knife?" he asked. When one student made a slicing motion this Kung Fu expert told him: "That's a good way to be killed." He then illustrated and debunked a typical knife stance seen on TV. "An attack with an overhand slash like that never happens except in the movies" he told the students. Then he showed the most common correct way to hold a knife, near the body.

"If a man with a knife attacked a karate Black Belt who should win?" he asked. When some of the students voted for the Black Belt, Master Pei set them straight. "Remember", he said, "the man with the knife, even without any knowledge of fighting, is still a more formidable foe than the martial arts person. If he also happens to possess knowledge of Oriental fighting he is unbeatable. And never forget, if the mugger has a gun there is no way, I repeat, **no way,** to defeat him unless by a miracle."

RULE NUMBER FIVE

Avoid becoming captive of a fixed idea on how to fight. Fifth Degree Aikido Master Richard Bowe best described this problem common to many martial artists: "Try throwing a roundhouse kick or a judo throw when cornered in a telephone booth. The late Bruce Lee was right when he said that a fighter should never become a 'programmed robot' ".

Master Bowe continued: "A few years ago the Russians swept the World Judo Championships. For the first time ever they took certain weight divisions that had been Japanese turf since the championships began. How did this come about? The Russians used some moves from Sambo! The Japanese, trained in the traditional judo way, were not responding correctly to the unorthodox maneuvers. That's why so many times one reads about a martial artist being badly injured or killed in an encounter with a street fighter. Often the one trained in the fighting disciplines is unprepared to fight someone who does not go into an accepted stance."

"The American martial artist should copy the Japanese players. As soon as they realized that the Sambo techniques had dethroned them they sent a number of their leading judokas to study the new art. At the next World Championships they resumed their rightful place as the world's leading judo power."

Master Bowe continued: "Many consider the nunchaku the ultimate fighting weapon. A Fifth Dan friend of mine said he would be able to defeat an opponent before he could take his nanchaku away. I disagreed, challenged him, and there was a small wager on the outcome. I threw my wallet at him! He was startled and went to grab it, by which time I was on top of him and was able to take the sticks away from him without getting hurt myself."

RULE NUMBER SIX

Even karate masters must break out of fixed fighting patterns. One very prominent Sensei came to assist me at an all-woman self-defense session by showing the women some supposedly workable maneuvers. I took him to a side room and demonstrated to him that some of his defense techniques were faulty because they did not work against me. He was flabbergasted!

Nevertheless, back on stage he insisted on showing the very techniques I had proved were ineffective. At one point he described a particularly impressive technique which featured a woman grabbing a man's hand and turning her back to him while twisting his arm. To show how easy it was the Master grabbed my hand, turned his back on me, and tried to twist my wrist. At first I refused to cooperate because I didn't want students to be misled into trying an ineffective retaliatory procedure that might very well result some day in their being killed. But I finally relented and allowed him to twist my hand so that he could save face.

RULE NUMBER SEVEN

Do not attend all-woman martial arts classes. Most women take up the combative arts because they fear being mugged, raped and/or being murdered by a man. Therefore it is useless for an instructor to train a woman to fight only another woman. A woman must learn to defend herself by practicing with a man. Otherwise the whole training program is an exercise in futility and self-delusion.

There is nothing wrong with having a female instructor but there must be male students in the class. If not the teacher fails to adequately prepare the woman for a realistic street situation where self-protection will be needed.

RULE NUMBER EIGHT

Never use an elbow to the gut or solar plexus when fighting heavier opponents. Diana Rigg, who played Emma Peele in the TV series *"The Avengers",* doubled up 250-pounders with ease. It simply can't be done.

RULE NUMBER NINE

Never throw those delights of the movie world, the high or flying kicks. As the late Bruce Lee said: "Any hood with even a smidgeon of knowledge of self-defense would immediately knock you off balance if you tried to use your legs in that fashion. When you're trading blows up close, the real Kung Fu calls for a wiser choice of attack. I never believe in jumping and kicking. My kicks, in actual Kung Fu, are not high but low, to the shin and groin."

RULE NUMBER TEN

Do not hesitate! Do what you have to do and do it instantly as if it were second nature. "He who hesitates is lost" is very apropos. Don't worry about injuries or death once the action starts. A strong positive attitude may get you out of the confrontation alive and unscathed.

RULE NUMBER ELEVEN

Stick to the basics. Forget the fancy techniques. As I mention elsewhere, Sensei Aaron Banks has said that the front kick and the reverse punch are the most potent weapons. Sensei Richard Mrofka concurs, saying that most tournament fighters would lose in street fights if they tried the off-the-wall techniques that gain judges approbation and the cheers of the unknowing crowds at tournaments. Remember, the trophy you are trying to win on the street is your life! That's too precious to gamble on trying to look showy.

RULE NUMBER TWELVE

In street fighting never turn your back for a back kick. Someone might stick a shiv in it.

RULE NUMBER THIRTEEN

Never depend on one single blow to put down an opponent. There are cases of attackers who, though mortally wounded, manage to fight on. A windmill of blows makes good sense. If it should become a fight to the death, and you fatally injure your opponent, you who have inflicted that fatal injury is not the victor if you yourself sustain a death-dealing blow from your dying adversary.

RULE NUMBER FOURTEEN

Don't try to foot-sweep someone who is much heavier than yourself. As I pointed out earlier, Sensei Numano said of this maneuver: "A tall man who is also heavy presents a problem. He may be so heavy that it is like attempting to topple the Empire State Building. Very difficult!"

Hopefully we've tossed away some of the myths and mysteries of the movies and the con-men. You the reader won't become Superman or Superwoman after practicing the techniques offered here, **but they might just save your life!**

CHAPTER TEN

<u>HOW TO FIGHT IN CLOSE QUARTERS</u>

For urban dwellers "I want to live!" is the name of the game. "To be or not to be" is more than a rhetorical question for people who live in constant fear of being mugged in elevators, held up in telephone booths, or murdered in back alleys.

Living in cities poses especially severe problems in survival tactics because the crime rate has more than doubled in the past decade. In fact the homicide rate alone has risen more than 100 percent in eight years. New York City annually has more fatalities from crime than the American Army suffered in any year of the Vietnam war! This is because of the 250,000 armed junkies roaming the Big Apple.

I am against meekly handing over money and valuables because surrender is no guarantee that you will be spared bodily harm.

Below are some self-defense techniques that can turn the tables on any aggressor in confined quarters. They make use of the five weapons you carry with you at all times: <u>two hands, two feet, and</u> <u>the knowledge within your brain</u>! The un-spectacular appearance of these close-quarter fighting maneuvers will not win you plaudits from the crowd, yet in a city's cramped spaces they may well save your life.

Of course, as with all other techniques in this book, you must practice them over and over until they become second nature. Remember, muggers ply their trade all the time, and their street-fighting experience makes them seasoned warriors who are not at all cowardly or they wouldn't be in their chosen profession. It's your life; it's their livelihood. Consider the alternatives. Never forget that there is no technique that can be effective unless the maneuvers become reflex action.

This is especially true when there is little room to move. When you are fighting in the wide open spaces there are opportunities to side-step and retreat and advance. In a telephone booth or elevator there is no such flexibility in tactics. The following eight scenarios will serve to illustrate many useful techniques.

You are alone in an elevator. The door opens and a menacing figure demands your money, and backs it up by choking you. You react instantly. Step back with your right foot and grab the attacker's arms by the elbows with a hard slapping motion. This will force him to release your throat. Release the attacker's arms, quickly moving your left hand down grasping his wrist firmly. Bring your knee up for a groin smash. Maintain your wrist hold and as the attacker falls finish with a right-hand reverse punch to the temple.

A word of general caution: Different individuals' threshold level for pain and punishment is highly variable. A blow that might fell one person may not even cause another to blink. Always be prepared to deliver an avalanche of blows and kicks.

A mugger grabs your wrist in an effort to wrench your arm around. Press your wrist against the attacker's thumb with a sudden jerk, and you will be released. If you press the other way against the fingers nothing will happen. If you have done it correctly, you now grab his wrist. To confuse him release his hand, grab him by the shoulders and push backwards, throwing him off balance both mentally and physically. With your left hand grab his right and throw a right hand punch to his chin, followed by a crushing right knee to the groin.

At a political meeting in a small room you get into a heated argument. Your opponent throws a left at your head. You defend with a high rising-block. <u>A good grasp of blocking is a must for personal self-defense.</u> (A prime example was the Ali-Foreman bout, after Ali was no longer able to "float like a butterfly and sting like a bee". Ali became the complete master of blocking techniques.) Your motto should be: <u>"Block and Counter Immediately"</u>. Step behind the attacker, grabbing him by the throat with your left hand. Block his vision with your right hand. Pull his neck back with a sudden jerk and move your fingers into his eyes. For an effective eye gouge press with your fingers from the sides of his nose into the corners.

A thug demands your money and grabs you by the right shoulder. You break his hold by smashing him in the jaw with a left-hand palm-heel strike, jolting his head backwards. With your right hand grab his Adam's apple and pull it. If that fails to quiet him, keep throwing blows to the head. Incidentally, a palm-heel strike is one of the most deadly of all karate blows.

An attacker grabs your wrists. Move your right foot back and with a sudden upward movement against his thumbs you break his hold. Move into the horse stance, bending your knees and lowering your butt as if you were riding a horse. Finish him off with a low backhand to the groin.

A thief grabs you by the left shoulder. With your right hand you strike him at his right elbow joint to break his hold. Maintain control of his right arm with your left hand. Slip your right leg behind his, grab his shoulders and push. Now, with his balance broken, twist your body to the right and push him over your leg and down. Finish with a barrage of kicks.

A thug grabs you by the shirt collar. Grab his arms at the elbows and push them together. Bring your knee sharply up into his groin, finishing with a back and forth double elbow strike to the face.

You're sitting at your friendly neighborhood bar having a quiet drink when a wise-guy throws a left at your face. You block, at the same time reaching for his head. Your right palm then strikes his jaw while your left hand is holding his head. The heel of your palm then rides up harshly against his lips and nose as your fingers form a "tiger's paw" into his eyes. Now grab his head behind the ears and gouge his eyes with your thumbs, pushing in and out. Then holding him with your left hand reach behind his back and throw an elbow smash to the throat. Your left arm is perfectly positioned for sweeping him off his stool with his right leg while wrenching his shoulder with a "wing lock". With his head held fast bring up a knee smash to his face. Then drive him to the floor with an elbow smash to the nape of his nick Grab his head and twist sharply against the flow of his fall, breaking it, and then smash his head against the floor. Finish with a knee drop to his face.

It's a good idea to rehearse these scenarios with a friend. Go very slowly at first, then increase speed as you gain confidence. Naturally, in practice you pull your blows, stopping just short of your target. If it is possible for you to attend a martial arts school please do so. It is the best life insurance you can buy.

CHAPTER ELEVEN

HOW TO KICK A MUGGER'S ASS

In this chapter I am going to offer suggestions for protecting yourself in a variety of real-life street-confrontation situations.

Always try to avoid unconsciously warning an opponent of your next move. This is known in sports parlance as "telegraphing". It refers to any move or mannerism that will reveal your intentions to your opponent before they are carried out. For example, instead of bringing your knee up before you are in striking range shuffle forward and then deliver the sharp knee kick. Or, if your opponent is still standing, bring your hand from your side without cocking your fist, so that you do not telegraph a blow. Then smash him with a back fist to the face.

Fake a reverse punch so that you can grab his jacket at the arm. Punch him under the arm. Then pull down on the same arm as he attempts to retreat. Punch him in the face again. Drive a roundhouse kick into his ribs. Quickly stomp the back of his knee which is closest to you forcing him to drop to the ground. Finish with a sharp kick to the chest.

You can also make a fake to the head with your lead hand. Follow with a second fake to his body with your pulled hand. As your opponent blocks fake again, to his body, and sweep his forward leg. As he hits the ground attack with punches to the face.

You fake a reverse punch so you can grab a thug's sleeve and deliver a kick, followed by a punch under his arm. Pull down on the same arm and as he retreats punch him in the face.

A thug approaches, and you cross-step to the rear. This should lead your opponent to believe you are about to attempt a side kick. You switch your attack to a back-hand strike that will usually score because you opponent's arm is low to block the anticipated side kick. As his arm begins to come up to block your already in-and-out backhand, strike with a reverse punch.

Typically a street bully will start off an attack with an intimidating move, such as a grab. You can easily halt the attack at this stage by bringing the arm on the side of the grab up and around the attacker's arm and under his armpit. At this point it only takes a little pressure on your part to break his arm. Now follow up with a palm-heel strike to the chin or bridge of the nose and you should easily be able to bring the man to the ground. Finish him with a punch to the ribs.

If an attacker grabs your wrist turn your hand until the palm faces out and immediately use your free hand to grab your opponent's hand between his thumb and forefinger. The twisting motion should have freed your hand, but if not the pressure applied on his hand will. A downward pressure with your first two fingers at the base of the palm while pushing inward and upward with your thumb will cause considerable pain. Maintaining pressure on his right hand, begin pressure on the inside of his elbow with your left. Stepping slightly to his outside, pushing down with your left hand and up with your right, you have him in a lock that will definitely quiet him!

An attacker grabs your wrist. Step in to loosen pressure and take hold of his wrist with your free hand, thumb on top. Bend slightly at the knee and lean in towards him, pushing his elbow and shoulder toward his head. Pressure is applied to his arm by the hand he is holding as well as the hand applying pressure to his wrist.

As an assailant grabs your right wrist with his left step back and bring your right hand up towards your face. Then place your left hand under his wrist with your thumb on top and fingers below. Bringing your held hand down and your other hand up will cause him to release his hold.

A thief grabs you by your jacket lapel and prepares to throw a knee kick. You step in and push his knee aside, wedging your fists between his arms, one from underneath and the other from above. Lift one hand you have wedged in to throw him off balance. Having trapped his hands by lifting one over the other you now grab the thief's hair. You then pull his head down and smash your knee into his face. Follow with a right elbow to the side of his head. Putting your body weight behind the elbow strike drive the assailant into the ground.

As a thug prepares to unleash a side thrust kick, start to take a step back. Move into a cat stance and simultaneously grab the mugger's ankle. Step out of the cat stance while pulling the thug off balance. Start to step forward while lifting the thug's leg. Complete your forward step to unbalance the mugger completely.

A mugger attempts to punch you in the face. Step to the side as you deflect his punch with an open hand block that you turn into a wrist grab. Stepping forward into a horse stance, while still holding the thug's wrist execute a hammer fist blow into his groin. Still holding the thug's wrist apply pressure to the elbow joint, effectively locking it into place. Continuing to apply pressure to the elbow joint force him to the ground.

A thug attempts to punch you. Step in and deliver a back-fist to his head, followed quickly by a back-fist to his groin. Repeat these two blows in rapid succession. Then an elbow to the midsection drives him backward over your out-stretched leg onto the ground. Finish with a kick to the throat.

You are menaced by a thief armed with a large knife. You grab the knife by the blade. You believe that it will not cut, so it will not happen. The power of your faith is all-important here. Twist the blade into him with your right hand and with the fingers of your left drill into his eyes. After the knife falls to the floor you rip out his Adam's apple while your right tears at his testicles.

An attacker threatens you with a club, forcing you into an on-the-knees pleading position in an effort to humiliate you. You dive for the attacker's ankle and effect an ankle throw by pressing very hard with your forefinger against a pressure point located just above the front of the ankle. The intense pain forces the attacker to go down. It must be remembered that there are different thresholds of pain. In some cases it might be better to forego the pressure point technique and simply grab the foe by the ankle and yank him off his feet.

Your attacker leads with a front snap kick. This is blocked at the ankle by your forward arm, which pushes the leg in and across your body. The leg is transferred to your rear arm which hooks under at the ankle and holds it high while you deliver a blow with the forward arm. Now drop your opponent to the ground by pressing up and back on his leg.

If a thug gets into a fighting stance, you drive a roundhouse kick into his ribs. Then stomp the back of the knee closest to you forcing the thug to drop to the ground. Finish with a sharp kick to his chest.

An assailant grabs you by the collar. You reach across with your right hand to grab his wrist and lock your hands behind it. Locking the blade of one hand above the wrist and the blade of the other beneath the joint of the elbow, exert enough pressure in opposite directions to break his arm at the wrist.

When a street thug grabs your collar with both hands he is setting himself up for an easy counter because both of his hands are occupied. A rapid combination of palm-heel strikes to the bridge of his nose, a punch to the solar plexus, and an elbow to the chin will do the trick in this situation.

A thug attacks you with a double frontal lapel hold. You extend your arms forward through the attacker's arms and grasp him by the biceps. Step forward and push him off balance and backwards with the forward energy of your body, as well as with your outstretched arms. Important: Keep your opponent's front leg in check in case he tries to slip in a kick or a knee.

If you are facing a thug and your position is such that you are in front of him, charge forward as he starts a kick. Before his leg is fully extended and has made contact, you scoop it up and step in with an elbow smash to the solar plexus. He goes down with you still in control of his leg.

You and a mugger square off. The thief, a karate student, starts a roundhouse kick. Before his leg is fully extended and has made contact, you scoop it and step in with an elbow smash to his face. The mugger is going down while you are still in control of his leg.

If a thug starts a kick and you are off to the side of him, charge forward. Your outstretched arm smashes into his neck, and you smash him down to the ground with a neck hold.

An attacker attempts a downward knife-hand strike. You move in with a close punch to the chest and a shuto to the back of his neck.

Using a minimum amount of movement you swivel to avoid a punch thrown by an assailant. You grab the punching arm with your left hand and pull him into a fore-knuckle punch to his vulnerable side.

As an attacker pushes you back grab his hand, drop down, and deliver a straight kick to his stomach. Then kick with your right leg to his groin. Then apply a leg-over arm-bar to throw the attacker to the ground. Keeping the arm tightly locked shoot a heel kick to the aggressor's head.

An attacker grabs your wrist. You bend your knees slightly and begin to twist out of his hold. You then grab his wrist. Keeping his palm up, bring his wrist around clockwise, pushing his elbow toward his rib cage and twisting his hand towards the floor, snapping his wrist and making the throw.

An attacker grabs your wrist. You pivot and extend your arm to the left pulling the attacker off balance and interrupting his line of force. You then sweep your arm down and up on your right side stopping it at the top of the arc. This dissipates any remaining force in the attacker's left arm and loosens his grip. At the top of the arc you grip the attacker's hand and use your thumb to apply pressure to the back of his hand between the thumb and forefinger. With a twist of the wrist you now have the attacker in a wrist-lock. Your remaining move is to come down on the back of his elbow with a forearm smash. In this forearm blow your fingers are spread wide which causes your forearm to become iron-hard.

The attack here is similar to the previous one except that the attacker grabs your sleeve instead of your wrist. The setup is the same with the wide sweeping arc, except that because of the looseness of the sleeve his grip is not released. This is used to your advantage when you continue the sweep, complete the circle, and finish with a successful wrist throw.

You are accosted by three thugs. As they near you, one steps out to confront you while the other two circle around to prevent your escape. You grab the first man's arm and strike quickly to the face with a straight punch. Almost at the same instant as your fist makes contact you strike out at the second man with a side kick to the groin. Before your leg even returns to the ground you are after the third man with a hammer fist to the head, finishing him off with a strike under the upper arm and an elbow to his shoulder blade. When facing a multiple attack situation you must strike hard and fast and then move on as quickly as you can.

Here is another three-against-one situation. This time the first attacker is on your left. The instant this man grabs you, whirl around breaking his half-tightened grip. Crouching low come up into the man with a punch to the midsection. As the second man shoots a roundhouse kick to your head you quickly strike out at his groin with a modified side kick, finishing with a reverse punch. By this time the third man has moved in behind you and has applied a choke hold. You shoot your fingers back into this man's eyes, grabbing his arm and throwing him to the ground. You finish him with a heel stomp to the head.

In a four to one scenario, you are attacked when going up a flight of stairs. As the first man attacks you block his punching arm and throw a strong back-fist to his head. As the second thief attacks hit him with a side kick that knocks him into the steps. As the third man begins his attack you block his front kick and strike to the back of his knee sending him down. The fourth man leaps at you with a lunge punch that you block. Then crouch and come in low with a punch of your own and throw a side kick to knock the man down. This all should give you a chance to get away.

Your best defense is a good offense. Here are a few techniques to keep an attacker at bay.

To defend yourself without really hurting an attacker, get him against a wall and place the side of your forefinger over his upper lip. Then shove upward under his nose. It's a painful hold that leaves your other hand free to do more harm if necessary.

You move in with a left back-fist with elbow raised and forward as a defense against a possible right hand counter. Pivot counterclockwise so that your right arm is forward, with elbow raised to prevent an attack to your upper body and head. Then strike with a right back-fist to the right temple of your opponent and drive a reverse punch into his throat.

Open up your drive with a reverse punch to the head to draw a thug's block. Then snap a hard ridge hand to the neck. Follow immediately with a second reverse punch to the throat and finish with a front kick to the midsection.

You throw a roundhouse kick which is blocked. Your opponent counteracts with a reverse punch. You slide back just out of reach and shoot out a side kick to the body. Reload and lash out with another roundhouse kick, forcing the thug to retreat.

You grab an attacker's jacket at the right shoulder with your right hand. Protecting your face with your free hand quickly move towards him. Keeping your face and body protected, and with a quick pivoting motion, throw him further off balance permitting you to secure an arm hold. Now, in full control, you grip his nose tightly and exert pressure on either the arm or the nose.

When you attack, extend your attacking arm at the same time as four forward-sliding front foot. Your left hand gently cancels your opponent's front hand. Then use your left hand to gently pull down and control your adversary's right arm. Throw a reverse punch to his face.

You can always trap your opponent by stepping on his foot. Grasp him and spin him around. Follow up with a roundhouse kick to his side, and finish him with a shuto to the back of his neck.

Only through practice and repetition will you become sufficiently proficient to protect yourself in these all-to-common street confrontations. As I said earlier, you must practice with a friend, carefully going through the techniques in slow motion. To become truly proficient your actions must become reflex.

The ability to block an opponent's blow and retaliate instantly is the sure-fire formula for success in any street encounter. To mix the ingredients successfully one must make the transition from blocking to throwing a blow smoothly with no mental hesitation.

All the moves must flow naturally from one to the other. **Often the only difference between the winner and the loser of a fight is the absence of indecision on the winner's part.**

CHAPTER TWELVE

<u>NEVER TOO YOUNG TO LEARN</u>

As a teacher of martial arts I have observed another aspect of self-defense training that is too often overlooked. Americans tend to think of martial arts as a chop-chop/kill-kill cult of Oriental crazies! The arts themselves are not considered to have any redeeming social value. The character development of the young student while in training and its effect on his everyday life is completely overlooked.

The youngster who has undergone such training is rewarded with the Golden Key of success in all facets of life. He has become endowed with the ability to shine in all areas of endeavor, be they the academic pursuits, sports, or the complex subtleties of social intercourse.

To become a champion it takes a kid who has the character and determination to stick to something until he has it mastered, but who is still never satisfied with the results. He must also have an almost abnormal desire to excel. He must be an individual who spends so much time on what he is doing that he lives a completely lopsided life, the kind of boy who is happy only when he is doing his own thing.

Finding a child of this type is equivalent to finding pure gold, because most of us are made of baser stuff. I believe the character improvement, reliability and stick-to-itiveness, and the sheer guts it takes to go out and face an opponent day after day is inestimable. Remember, the greatest thing about any martial art is that it is a completely individual exercise in self-development. There is no possible self-shirking alibi, no excuse the "other guy" fumbled the ball.

Nowadays youngsters scream about the loss of individuality and they go about asking questions like: "Who am I?". If they are curious to find out the answers let them enter any one of the martial arts and discover, when they face their opponents and are scored upon, that there is nobody to blame but themselves. They will know they are losers because they didn't practice hard enough. They should not accuse their parents or society. It was because they themselves didn't do their martial arts homework.

That's why I believe the character building aspects of the martial arts are the greatest in the world. And when parents are fortunate to have children who can benefit from a martial arts regime they should be extremely grateful. The very qualities of perseverance, the ability to come back time after time after a defeat, to take a blow without whimpering: **These are the marks of a winner in every aspect of life.**

The loser usually has a completely different viewpoint. I'm not saying conditions over which we have no control may not completely alter our lives. What I am saying is that if it takes character to succeed in a certain situation, the martial arts trained boy or girl will be successful and win out over those who were not fortunate enough to possess such training.

The discipline involved in performing a specific task, carrying it out carefully and well and following it to completion, builds character and therefore constitutes invaluable training for adulthood.

CHAPTER THIRTEEN
<u>BEAT THE SCHOOLYARD BULLIES</u>

The following eleven scenarios are often encountered in schoolyard fights.

On the street it's called the old "sucker punch". It's a favorite of playground bullies. The bully cocks his arm ready to throw the punch. You step back, and block with your left hand. Follow with a short right hand punch to the bully's stomach. Grab his arm and put your right leg behind his forward leg, and sweep him onto the ground. Follow with a punch to the ribs. Strike repeatedly.

A bully approaches with evil intentions. Grab his hair, drop down, and put your right hand directly behind his knee. Pulling his hair back, step back with your left foot, pulling him down. Follow through with right punches to his ribs.

Two bullies approach their mark from behind, with one putting him in a rear stranglehold. With his right hand the victim reaches back and gives the strangler a powerful groin squeeze which forces him to release his pressure and allows escape. As the second bully wades in he is smashed with a front kick to the groin. With both bullies stunned it is easy for the victim to escape.

Two bullies begin throwing reverse punches aimed at their victim's face. These are stopped effectively with a double high- rising-block with both arms. A swift kick to the groin disables one attacker. He then grabs the second attacker's arms stretching his body and pushing hard, throwing him to the ground . Finish with kicks to any vulnerable part.

A bully twists his victim's arm behind his back. To break the hold the victim brings his right foot forward and bends his knees. Pressing against the bully's thumbs with a sudden snap he twists his body and breaks the hold completely. A reverse punch to the bully's face ends the fight.

A bully begins to throw a right-hand punch at your face. Execute a high block with your left hand against his right forearm. As you do this, move your left foot forward and slightly to the left. Pull the attacker's right hand sharply downward and towards his left rear. Simultaneously shove hard against the bully's left shoulder with your right hand, which will cause the bully to be leaning off balance to the side and rear. Continue to push and use your right leg to sweep the bully's right leg out from under him. Finish with sharp kicks to any vulnerable points.

A bully grabs you from the front in a bear hug. He has your arms pinned to your sides. Before he has time to tighten his hold lift your arms and strike hard into his sides with the edges of your two hands, aiming just above the belt line. This should stun the bully long enough to escape the grip. If you still find your arms pinned strike him hard in the groin with either or both knees.

A bully grabs your left wrist with his right hand. Extend your left foot slightly forward, clench your fist at your waist, and deliver punches to his Adam's apple and jaw.

If a bully knocks you down all is not lost. As he steps towards you, place your right foot behind his right heel. Turning on your right side, supported by your right elbow, deliver a stomping type kick to the bully's knee with your left arch or heel. As you drive his knee backwards draw his right foot towards you, pulling it with his entrapped foot. The combined push at the knee and pull at the heel drops the bully to the ground. If you have kicked hard enough his knee will be broken. As he falls to the ground you can regain your feet and deliver powerful kicks to end the fight.

When both of the combatants in a schoolyard fight have karate training the situation can get dangerous. Given two combatants with equal determination the one with the best techniques will always come out on top. One combatant, A, moves forward and throws a reverse punch which is blocked with a high rising block movement. Combatant B follows through with a right front kick, but A stops it with a left hand inside block, pushing B's foot to the side. While B's foot is still in the air A foot-sweeps B's left leg with his right foot, dropping B. Then A jumps on B and finishes him with a punch to the chin.

Two boys square off in a fighting stance. Opponent A throws a reverse punch at opponent B, who stops it with a high rising block, keeping the punch from striking his face. Opponent B throws a sharp open-hand strike (the shuto, or chop) stopped by A with a left-hand high rising block keeping the blow away from his temple. A follows through with a front kick, and unleashes a stomp kick. B steps back on his right foot and throws a roundhouse kick at A's head, who manages to stop it with a high rising block. A grabs B tightly by the throat, but B breaks this stranglehold by striking sharply with both arms up and outward. B now brings his hands down and under A's arms past his elbows, and ends the fight with a knee smash to A's groin.

As with all moves described in this book, practicing in slow-motion with a partner is the best way to learn the nuances of various martial arts self-protection techniques. After a while practice at faster speeds, of course pulling the punches and kicks. The key is always repetition. Once moves have become reflex you are in a fine position to protect yourself from any bully foolish enough to challenge you!

If you possibly can, get enrolled in a professional martial arts class. Honor and obey your instructor. Follow your instructions, complete your repetitions, and **stick with it.** You'll be glad you did.

And never forget, it is **always** better to **avoid** a fight, and running away as fast as possible has saved many a broken bone or tooth.

There is no shame in avoiding a fight if you possibly can.

CHAPTER FOURTEEN
<u>HOW TO AVOID BEING RAPED</u>

The man's fingers made a clutching motion towards the frail looking blonde's hair. She stopped him with a rising block and a quick front kick to the groin. As he doubled up, her knee squashed his nose flat. She grabbed him by the ear, jerking his head down while keeping up a steady drum roll of knee smashes to his battered face. As he sank unconscious to the floor she rubbed her hands together gleefully, and with the triumphant air of one who had done a job well she exclaimed: "Karate training does it every time!"

You've come a long way baby, but not **that** far. Although martial arts instructors, women's liberation groups, the movies and television try to present the above version of how a trained fighting woman would respond to an attack, unfortunately, in real life, it rarely if ever happens that way.

Here is a more realistic picture of what might have happened. Despite the late hour our young blond sauntered through the tree-shaded lawn of the college campus with a certain degree of complacency. In one hand she held the tip of her green belt wound around her karate gi, while in the other she clutched a newly-won first-place trophy. Suddenly a dark shape materialized. A muscular arm was wrapped around her throat and her body was yanked brutally back towards the bushes. Her **only** thought was: "God help me". Petrified with fright she forgot everything she had ever learned about self-defense, and was repeatedly and brutally raped.

Martial arts training notwithstanding, no technique is better than the person using it. For instance, an individual can practice jabbing a finger into an eye any number of times, but if the potential victim is psychologically unprepared to actually perform this rather grisly task then this training in self-defense is completely wasted. How many women or men after even three years of practice are prepared to permanently blind another human being?

Army tests have shown that a goodly portion of American soldiers in battle were not firing at the enemy, but aiming their rifles at the sky! Should we expect the female of the species to be more deadly in a life and death situation?

According to Dr. Martin Symonds, an N.Y.U. psychiatrist, the normal reaction to a rape attack is paralyzing fear. He says: "To understand why victims frequently offer little resistance during a rape it is crucial that the rape be viewed not as a sex crime but as a crime of violence. The common denominator of all violent crime is the terrorization of the victim to insure immediate subjugation."

He goes on to say that a victim's typical reaction to a crime of violence is shock and disbelief. This fright-panic response is especially true when the individual believes that their life is in danger. Often what the psychiatrist calls a "psychological infantilism" occurs in which the victim's efforts are directed at remaining externally calm with little energy for resistance. "The profound terror makes the victim childlike in their behavior". He called it an "act of submission" that could inhibit the actions of some aggressors, but in general "rapists are alienated to the victim's needs."

"Only one of 4,000 cases reported to the police department," Symonds said, "indicated that there was an act of resistance." Symonds has counseled such victims who were so glade to be alive that "some have sat down on the street and cried with joy, feeling that the attacker had given them back their lives. Some were so grateful that they refused to testify for the prosecution. I'm not surprised by submission, but by resistance", said Symonds, indirectly attacking the societal attitude that rape is somehow the woman's fault. The doctor also said that early life patterns would determine whether a victim might resist, and that such acts of retaliation are repugnant to many women who were without early exposure to violence.

And therein we have the crux of the matter. How can a few hours a week of martial-arts training erase years of conditioning?

Among my many female students, two, with vastly different backgrounds, come to mind. One was a group of child psychologists with white upper-middle-class backgrounds. As individual students they had been thrown out of a number of dojos, being labeled "undesirables". They were reluctant to use the techniques they were paying to learn.

The other students came from the ghetto, and were the so-called "culturally deprived". Nevertheless, within eight weeks after starting training these ladies were beating the crap out of their husbands and boyfriends during their squabbles. I taught exactly the same techniques to both groups. One group could effectively utilize my instruction. The other obviously could not. What was the difference? The members of the "deprived" class had been battling for survival since childhood. The others were a product of the protected, serene upbringing of typical middle-class white America.

When a physically insecure female student enters a dojo, if it is a tough, demanding school, she may quickly lose heart and abandon the class. On the other hand, if the school is too soft (and this tends to be true of women's classes, where giggles and laughter prevail) then she will not get authentic or even helpful martial-arts training. Students approach this latter kind of training with a casual attitude and describe it as "fun". I submit that a subject that is intended to protect a woman's life is **not** fun, nor should it be. Any student who is not willing to accept the necessary discipline and hard work to achieve proficiency is wasting her time.

According to Dr. Symonds, "Rapists know quite well that a torrent of verbal abuse accompanied by threats of violence will usually stun victims into shock and submission." Given this condition the unprepared victim becomes desperately concerned with her health and her life. She's willing to give the attacker anything as long as she's not hurt.

The psychiatrist said that there are two types of rapists, the compulsive and the predatory. "The compulsive rapist is acting out the symbolic gratification of deep-seated and unresolved sexual problems. He violates the rules of criminal behavior by talking with the victims, losing his anonymity. He often returns to the scene of the crime in an attempt to see the victim again because he is trying for an illusion of a relationship. His goal seems to be for the victim to 'give herself to him' ".

"The predatory rapist, by contrast, is intent only on ripping off the victim, taking her 'property, pride and body' ". Dr. Symonds said that they are "impulsive individuals with little or no emotional reserve, and demand no symbolic acting out on the woman's part." He went on to say that there is some overlap in behavior patterns between the two types, but what they have in common is the use of terror to subjugate their victim.

To follow the line of least resistance can be a trap from which there is no escape. One has only to remember that the eight nurses killed by Richard Speck could easily have overpowered their killer if they had been psychologically trained to defend themselves. This is especially true with 9 to 1 odds in their favor. Only one nurse had sense enough to hide. All of these young women were well educated, but their reasoning was faulty. They followed the theory of "talk your way out of the situation", even though more often than not this doesn't work. The truth is that most of the time the woman has nothing to lose by resisting, and it might just save her life.

Many years ago in a small New England town my mother was working as a nightclub singer. She took the precautionary measure of having herself driven to the train station by a policeman. En route he suddenly pulled off the road into the woods, took out his revolver, cocked it, pressed it against her head and threatened to rape her. He said if she resisted he would kill her.

My mother replied resolutely that as far as she was concerned he could squeeze the trigger, because as a devout Roman Catholic she believed that if she gave in she would lose her immortal soul. She recounted that the policeman put away his revolver and held on to the steering wheel of the patrol car, his whole body shaking. After he recovered somewhat, he said he would drive her to the station, but if she ever told anybody about the incident or came back to the town he would kill her. Realizing that no one would take the word of a woman against that of a police officer, she let him drive her to the station. Perhaps if she had submitted and allowed him to rape her, he, fearing apprehension and punishment, might have felt it necessary to kill her to assure her silence and his safety.

Proponents of the "submission theory" may say that compliance is best, and that if a woman fights back she might be killed. Of course this can occur, but what they fail to recognize is the fact that many attackers are also turned on sexually by the very **thought** of killing her. Tests of semen on the underpants of Richard DeSalvo illustrated this fact.

In my karate classes and rape-prevention clinics I have always stressed that the willing victim learns that an umbrella of talk will not save her from harsh reality.

Any expert, whether Black Belt or professional boxer, will agree that mental preparation is at least 90 percent of any fighter's equipment. Unfortunately, mental preparation is precisely what is lacking when it comes to the self-defense training of women. Whether it is a class where the instructor gives only lip service to the training of females, or an all-woman class where everything is polite, both fail miserably in <u>the main objective of preparing the woman to go out there and really fight.</u> In a martial arts class true equality of the sexes should prevail. That means that women get as black and blue as the men. Just as a boy needs to be roughed up a bit before he becomes a man, a girl needs the same treatment to help her make the same transition into womanhood.

Some instructors, perhaps from a misguided sense of gallantry, maintain that a female should not free-fight during her menstrual period. This ignores the whole point of her lessons which is to train her to defend herself at <u>all</u> times.

If a woman (or a man for that matter) finds a school where the Sensei has a background that includes street-fighting experience, she's in luck. Why study with someone who has only read about those confrontations you might someday face? Teachers who work, or have worked, as bouncers are also recommended. I'm also against women flocking to classes run by female Green Belts rather than one presided over by a teacher of Black Belt status. Women's Libbers might say this is male chauvinism, but as a woman you are training to defend yourself against men as well as other women. Moreover, a Black Belt simply has more experience and expertise than a practitioner of lesser rank. <u>Insist on a Black Belt to teach you.</u>

So how can a woman defend herself? Most women do not realize that they can put up an excellent defense if only they make up their minds to do so. They are probably carrying in their handbags such implements as a ball-point pen or nail file, both good for jabbing into an eye and blinding. A comb or key can also blind. I do not advise ever slashing an attacker across the face. It simply does not stop an attacker. If a woman is going to resist, which I strongly advocate, then she should offer an effective defense. Jabbing a nail file up a man's nose, for example, is far more painful and effective than using it to slash his face.

If a woman has sharp, strong teeth she can bite off an attacker's nose. Even better than that, the skin at the hollow of the neck is very thin and can easily be pierced, much as a plastic bag, with just the fingers and nails. It should be ripped open to allow direct access to the windpipe. The blood vessels in the neck, such as the carotid artery and the jugular vein can be best accessed with the teeth. These vessels are just under the skin, and the object is not to cut off the circulation but to tear them out. The front teeth should sink into the skin and vessels, and the woman should pull her head away with a violent jerk, leaving a killer wound.

Alternately, a woman can use her thumb and forefinger which should be driven into the attacker's throat with a tong-like grip on the horns of the thyroid cartilage just above the larynx (voice box). Firm digital pressure is applied and maintained until the attempted rapist collapses. If the woman feels she cannot keep up the pressure long enough she can always rip out his Adam's apple.

Violent? Yes indeed. Potentially life-saving? Yes indeed. Teachable? Yes indeed. Doable? That is entirely up to you, the potential rape/murder victim.

CHAPTER FIFTEEN

SELF-DEFENSE FOR THE HANDICAPPED & ELDERLY

The paralyzed moved, the deaf heard, and the sightless could see! So it appeared when the double amputee in his wheelchair fought back against two husky men. As one man aimed a kick at him, the disabled man grabbed the other's leg and with a sudden twist sent that attacker to the floor. There was a sharp intake of breath from the observers. Then pandemonium reigned as the amputee gripped the armrests on his chair and launched himself into the air, his stumps hitting the other man in the groin. As the attacker hit the floor the amputee jumped on top of him and smashed his gigantic fist into the other's face.

There was reverential silence as if the scene was being reenacted in a cathedral. In a sense this was a religious ceremony. The rapt patients in the Veteran's Hospital were whole again, living vicariously as they got in their longed for licks against the world that had tried to destroy them. A miracle had occurred in the person of Ted Vollrath. Later, every ward and corridor in the medical center buzzed with the talk about "the most amazing man alive".

Vollrath is breaking a barrier of prejudice. The world's most unusual karateka, he completely shatters the conventional role of the handicapped. Often the handicapped are given sympathy, but seldom are they allotted their share of respect from their fellow humans.

After a near-fatal injury in the Korean war, and 83 separate operations that involved removing both legs and a lung, most people would give up and call it the finish of a life. Vollrath might have attempted to live the miserable, frustrating existence of a bedridden invalid. Certainly no one in his condition had ever before attempted to live the life of a professional athlete. Vollrath attempted, and succeeded. He learned to get maximum use out of his damaged body. His message to other handicapped persons is: "Achieve full efficiency. And tell healthy persons to go to Hell when they begin to dwell on their limitations."

Ted says: "I started in karate for the purpose of seeing if a handicapped person could participate in the martial arts field. My greatest ambition in life is to prove to doctors and all others that someone like me can perform and be recognized as a contributor to mankind, not just a symbol of pity."

To become a useful member of society once again, Vollrath began performing services for others, first as a Cub Scout leader, then as coach of a championship "Pony League" baseball team. The boys soon found out that Vollrath's theme was: "If you have an alibi, don't use it." It is little wonder that his young charges ended the season with a 15 – 1 record!

But he was still not satisfied with his accomplishments. He did not want to remain an interested observer for the rest of his life. He wanted to be an active participant, but that was easier dreamed than achieved.

Laws ban discrimination because of race, sex, creed, or age, but the handicapped are fair game for everyone's prejudices. One karate instructor told him flatly that he was unwelcome in the class. Another Sensei conned him out of his money but gave him no instructions.

He relates his ordeal: "In the very beginning I was not accepted by a high-ranking Black Belt as a man capable of performing adequately because I was legless. I attended classes for about three months but received no personal attention to encourage me to continue. I only participated in the formal exercises. I was left by myself with no one to even see if I was capable of taking part in the instructions. I was becoming discouraged until Jim Clark and Rick Matthews invited me to attend their classes. This was the beginning of my new life! Jim and Rick knew I wanted to learn, and I knew I had it in me to learn. Also, I was interested in proving the other instructors were wrong. It took time and patience and special people to help me accomplish what I have today."

"We worked together as a team. We began from the floor, until we realized how important my wheelchair was. It gives me height and mobility, and the chair itself can be used as a deadly weapon in that the arms are detachable and can be used as weapons. We discovered how various moves can be made from the wheelchair. At times Jim sat in it and tried to perform acts from my position. It was hard and steady work for all of us."

In eight years, by dint of grueling labor, Vollrath achieved the rank of Eighth Degree Black Belt in Isshin Ryu, Second Degree Black Belt in Shorin-ji Ryu, and First Level Kung Fu. These are amazing accomplishments seldom achieved by able bodied individuals. Paraplegic Preston Carter originated the "Martial Arts for the Handicapped Federation" (MAHF), but Vollrath, leaping from his wheelchair, became the organization's symbol of resistance to the pressures of society.

In a recent interview Vollrath said: "Teaching the handicapped is what I'm here for." He does not offer false rewards. His tests for higher belt ranks are just as strenuous as those for the able-bodied, though within the limitations of the individual student.

For those who claim that his high ranks were earned because his instructors felt sorry for him, he replies: "Contrary to many remarks that have been made, I'd like to say that I have worked as hard, if not harder, than any other Black Belt that I have ever met to achieve my ranks. I wasn't given token gifts. I had to perform every kata to reach my ranks, and likewise every kumite. I wasn't shown favoritism, though I cannot forget that without Senseis like Jim Clark and Rick Matthews none of this would have been possible."

When asked if he felt other disabled persons could follow his example he answered: "I don't recommend that everyone who is handicapped should try to overcome his helplessness by entering the martial arts. But I do recommend that every incapacitated person get involved in life in some way, even if it is only to go outside and look at the sun and <u>thank God to be alive."</u>

"Karate is excellent training and exercise for those who are handicapped and have an interest in the martial arts, providing their personal physician and handicap allow such activities. Encouragement and communication between handicapped people and society is recommended to overcome that feeling of helplessness and despondency regardless of what they undertake. Most people forget that I have no legs because I enjoy life to the fullest. After all, I only lost my legs, not my mind! I feel I have a lot to offer society."

He added: "I want to educate other Senseis in helping those disabled persons who are interested in the martial arts. I want them to make personal appearances at children's hospitals, VA hospitals, and rehabilitation centers across the country. I want to see them on TV, and with groups of karateka on tour."

Vollrath hunts, fishes, and is the Sensei of three dojos in the Harrisburg, Pennsylvania area. A proud father of four, he credits his wife with giving him the moral support needed to reach his goals, one of which was to be the first man to gain a Black Belt while confined to a wheelchair.

When asked what he would do today if attacked, Vollrath replied: "In a frontal approach I'd turn my body sideways, leaving as little a target as possible. I would let the attacker become the aggressor. The closer he comes to me the more advantage I have. In the case of a kick instead of hand techniques I can upset him to the ground and leap from the wheelchair and finish the job. Size doesn't make a difference when he is standing. His groin is my target area. After bringing him to his knees it's his face, and on the ground it's the end! I can even kick an attacker by raising myself on the arms of the wheelchair and sweeping my stumps into his groin. I could also reverse my position in the wheelchair and do a handstand and kick him in the face with my stumps. This is usually too much of a surprise for him to continue!"

The following are some maneuvers that other handicapped persons or the elderly can use. Because of the wide diversity of disabilities, all of these techniques may not apply to all situations.

An excellent self-defense weapon for the handicapped is an umbrella on which you have fastened a hunting arrowhead on the tip. Holding the umbrella with both hands thrust as hard as you can. This is guaranteed to discourage any attacker if you hit him in an exposed area such as his face.

Another sure-fire self-defense weapon, one which is perfectly legal, is the yawara stick. If you can't purchase one, any small tubular stick six inches in length will suffice. The stick is held in a clenched grip protruding from both sides of the fist. Lay the stick across the palm of the hand at the base of the fingers and tightly clench the fist around it. The thumb is right across the finger tips pointing towards the outside edge of the hand. The wrist muscles should be tense. This grip is used in chopping, slashing and stabbing strikes.

There are twenty-one important targets for this weapon: **1.** Adam's apple; **2.** Soft muscle centered directly under the chin; **3.** Temple; **4.** Neck muscle at the side of the windpipe; **5.** Delicate bone between the nose and upper lip; **6.** Mastoid bone behind the ear; **7.** Base of the skull; **8.** Prominent vertebra at the base of the neck; **9.** Breast bone; **10.** Directly under the bottom rib; **11.** Solar plexus; **12.** Soft muscle between the neck and the collar bone; **13.** Instep; **14.** Knee cap; **15.** Inner thigh; **16.** Lower abdomen; **17.** Spinal column between the shoulder blades; **18.** Base of the spine; **19.** Kidneys; **20.** Directly behind the knee; **21.** Achille's heel.

For those confined in a wheelchair the following techniques can be used with the yawara stick in actual situations:

While seated next to the invalid, an attacker unexpectedly pulls him in by the lapel to deliver a punch. The invalid turns towards the mugger and pins his hand tightly to his own chest. Simultaneously the invalid brings the stick up behind the attacker's elbow joint. Still holding the mugger's hand tightly against his own chest the invalid smashes down against the target area of the attacker's outside elbow joint. This blow will force the attacker to the ground and may break the elbow joint.

An attacker catches the invalid in a painful arm bar from the side. To relieve the pressure and pain the invalid shifts his weight towards the mugger's body. This move brings him into striking position. Now the invalid moves slightly forward and swings the stick upward in a stabbing blow to the attacker's eye, crushing it.

Even a rolled-up newspaper or a book can serve as a weapon. Thrust the newspaper into the face, eyes, or under the chin, as well as into the solar plexus and groin. With two hands you can bring a book up under an attacker's throat or down the side of the face. Try jabbing a corner of the book directly into the attacker's eyes. Those who are obliged to walk with the aid of a cane should not despair. The stick can be a very powerful weapon, second only to the sword if one knows what to do with it.

Say an attacker seizes your left lapel. Swing the cane, which you are holding in your right hand, over the top of his wrist. Grip the cane with both hands and press down. When he has lost his balance, draw back with your right hand and push forward with your left in such a way that the lower half of the cane strikes the left side of the attacker's head. At the same time deliver a front kick to his groin.

As an alternative to the above, you could strike the attacker on his left side with the upper half of the cane. At the same time rotate your right hand in towards your body so as to strike the side of his face with the lower half of the cane. Almost immediately swing the cane around to a position from which you can smash his wrists from beneath. Deliver a finishing kick to the groin.

If an attacker should grasp both of your shoulders from behind, rest the head of the cane on your shoulder. Swing your body around and drive the head of the cane into his windpipe. As he flinches, lower the cane and drive a horizontal blow to his testicles.

As with all of the techniques in this book, it takes practice and many repetitions over time for the moves to become reflex.

Remember, a handicap does not have to mean helplessness.

CHAPTER SIXTEEN

<u>OUT OF SHAPE? OUCH!!!</u>

The   heavyset thirty-five year old Black Belt shot his foot up for a high leg stretch, shot out a roundhouse kick, shuttered and collapsed. After being rushed to the hospital it was learned that this man of Dan rank had not only dislocated his hip but also torn a groin muscle and thrown his back out of alignment! This misfortune occurred because the Black Belt had not sufficiently warmed up. He was not in shape.

Warm-ups are important for everyone, but especially for older individuals. Though we over-thirty athletes don't like to admit it, it takes us ten times as long to be ready for our sport when compared to a teenager. Those of us who have passed the age of thirty-nine find that the warm-up period takes up fully half of our workout time. Nevertheless, with all our preparation, torn and pulled muscles continue to plague us. This loss of resilience does not apply to practitioners of karate alone but to all older athletes.

Professional football players, for example, are notorious for taking all sorts of muscle relaxing drugs before a game to insure increased protection against muscle-related injuries.

It is well documented that after the middle twenties the muscles, sinews and cartilages begin to degenerate. The exigencies of life in general cause us to become more tense. This condition is aggravated if in addition one now worries about advancing years and declining powers. Thus, limbering-up exercises become of the utmost importance. Never is it more true that an ounce of prevention is worth a pound of cure!

Let's examine a number of exercises that should be considered for warm-up prior to **any** strenuous exercise or competition, and for keeping in shape in general:

NECK EXERCISE

A good way to relieve tensions is to slowly move your hear back and forth, side to side, and all the way around in a circular motion. Repeat this procedure at least ten times

SHOULDER EXERCISE

Raise your arms as high as they can go, then rotate them as fast as you can forward and backward. Repeat this procedure at least ten times.

BACK EXERCISE

Touch your toes and then lean backwards as far as you can go the other way. Now raise your hands over your head and stretch your upper body to each side without bending your knees and hip joint. Repeat this procedure three times.

HIP EXERCISE

With your arms out to the side, raise the fore-finger on each hand and swing your body around with your eyes following the finger as far back as it will go without moving your feet. Then swing to the other side. Repeat ten times. This is a great technique for flexibility and it will give you a hip movement that is second to none!

BODY TWIST

Twist your body from left to right with your arms at low, middle or high level. As you circle around you relax your torso and knees.

Perform the same basic exercise by moving the hips back and forth, from side to side, and then rotate in a circular motion. Repeat at least five times. If you are required to make a sudden twist you will be less likely to injure yourself.

SQUATS

Squats have come under fire from a number of medical persons as being injurious to your knees. For this reason I do not include this exercise as a recommended part of the warming-up process.

STRETCHES

A good way to stretch your tendons is to point your toes up when stretching your leg for a front kick. Put the outer edge of your foot up for the side kick. It is important to keep your supporting foot flat on the floor.

PUSHUPS

The pushup is a tremendous exercise whether it is done with one hand or two, using the palms, the first two knuckles, or for the virtuoso performer, the fingertips! What is most important is to make sure that the entire body moves up and down in a straight line. Repeat ten to twenty times.

SIT-UPS

The best way to get rid of that spare-tire around the middle is to do a number of sit-ups every day. Do as many as you can within your comfort level.

BACK STRENGTHENING

With a friend, who is about the same height and weight as you, stand back to back. Link arms, then one, then the other, lifts his partner's body off the floor. When lifting be **certain** to bend the knees.

SPECIAL SPLIT

With your legs apart as far as possible grab both ankles with your hands and touch the ground with your head. This procedure strengthens the legs, groin, and back of the thighs. Repeat ten times.

LOWER ABDOMEN

From a prone position raise your feet five inches above the ground and hold. Keep your hands under your hips to ease the strain on your lower back. Now separate your legs, bring them back together, hold once more and return to the starting position. To further strengthen the lower abdomen, rotate your legs to the right, bring them back up to complete 180 degrees, and then start to come down on the left side.

LEG STRETCH

Sitting on the floor stretch your legs as far apart as possible. Then have a friend push your body forward. Repeat ten times. Then have your friend push you to the left ten times, and then to the right ten times.

GROIN STRETCH

If you have only ten minutes a day for stretching, this is the best exercise for that all-important groin muscle. Sit on the floor, knees bent, and with your elbows try to press your knees into the ground. Then relax the muscles by shaking your legs. Repeat this procedure one-hundred times.

NECK ISOMETRICS

Put your hands in back of your neck, press, then relax. Repeat this ten times. Clench your hands in front of your head, push forward and then relax. Repeat ten times. These exercises will strengthen your neck. Another exercise for this area is to put your hands on the sides of your head and push your head against your hands. Relax and repeat ten times.

JAW STRENGTHENING

To strengthen the muscles of your jaw, chew chewing-gum frequently.

RELAXING

One of the best ways to learn how to relax until point of contact with your target is to begin with the stretching exercises. A good example is the split. Stretch your legs as far as you can extend them. Then make a momentary inward pulling motion. Repeat five times in that position, then straighten up. Repeat the entire procedure ten times. **CAUTION: If you feel any pain or heat stop immediately.** An unpleasant sensation means that you have pulled or torn a muscle. Observe this rule when stretching other parts of the body as well.

Follow this same procedure but with your arms fully extended. Press your fist into a wall, tense, and putting all of your weight behind this maneuver Kia silently. Hold the position for a second and then relax. Repeat at least ten times.

HAND CONDITIONING

This is an important part of self-defense training. **WARNING**: If you wish to play a musical instrument, type, or become a mechanic do not practice these exercises! They will inevitably cause a significant loss of finger dexterity. To toughen up your fingers, thrust them into a pail of sand. Repeat this at least ten times a day. Pound the makiwara board with punches repeatedly.

To illustrate the possible extreme consequences of over-rigorous hand conditioning, many years ago I had occasion to lunch with one of Japan's most celebrated karate masters. He was well known for his awesome punching power. His hands had become so deformed due to the wrong conditioning exercises that he was unable to manipulate chopsticks or even use a knife and fork! He pointed out one of his knuckles that was actually covering two fingers and explained that this deformity was the sorry consequence of faulty training.

The hand exercises described herein will not do that much damage, but they will definitely cause a loss of dexterity.

CHAPTER SEVENTEEN

<u>KEEN ADVICE FROM THE MASTERS</u>

The name "Yamaguchi" has become synonymous with karate. There is hardly a martial artist anywhere in the world who has not heard of "The Cat", Gogen Yamaguchi, head of Goju-Kai Karate-Do in Japan. His oldest son Gosei assumed the leadership of American Goju-Kai Karate-Do here in the States. Here is what he has to say about the effectiveness of karate techniques:

"Too many people in the U.S. are trying to attract the public by presenting karate as an exotic, avant-garde kind of thing. They tell the public that karate is a secret and mysterious Oriental form of self-defense. This is very misleading since, in my opinion, there's no such thing as a deadly or secret technique in karate. All of the principles and movements of karate can be proven scientifically through physics and biology."

"Now, if you had an opponent up against a wall where there was no way he could move back, and then you delivered a punch or kick, the chances are that the blow could cause death. But under normal fighting conditions such power in a technique doesn't exist, unless you catch your opponent right on the spot and completely off guard."

"People in karate don't trust or respect each other, not only in Japan or the U.S. but everywhere in the world. They have too much pride in their own art and reject others if they use a different kind of kick or punch. But any kind of kick is effective to a certain degree. For example, if I see some kind of spinning round kind of kick I cannot say that it isn't effective. Even though we, in Goju karate, don't use a kick like that it doesn't necessarily mean that there aren't other kinds of techniques which might also be used with just as much effectiveness."

"I think that the more a man becomes familiar with other modes of fighting, the better off he will be. This is not to say that he should forsake karate for something else, but he should learn how to adapt the principles of karate to other ways of fighting. This is where real understanding of karate and one's self comes in. Sometimes it isn't an easy thing to do, let alone accept."

"Since the world has been brought closer together through transportation and communication the fighting attitudes and methods of the world have become more complex and have encompassed more realms and approaches. For example, if a karateka fights a karateka, he will know basically what to expect and how to counterattack, and so on. But if a karateka fights a boxer or a wrestler his techniques are more difficult to apply because he is facing an opponent who uses different techniques from the universal art. It belongs to humanity, not just to the Japanese or Okinawans. Once one realizes this, it's foolish to assume that the art must be practiced in America exactly as it is in Japan. It must be adaptable enough to suit the mentality of the people who are practicing it."

Sensei Yamaguchi told this to David Cox for an article published in 1971. Back in 1963 Bruce Lee wrote a book titled: "*Chinese Gung Fu*". He had this to say about the effectiveness of kicks in a street encounter:

"The kick, especially in the Northern clans of Kung Fu, is a best means of attack, however, they too warn of the danger of using them recklessly. It is a fact that the legs are much more powerful and have a longer reach than the hands, but we must also consider that when we lift one leg and kick our whole balance is involved."

"In training, kick as high as you can. But in combat kick as fast as you can and don't pass over the belt. This is a saying I often teach to my students. In my school our kicks seldom pass over the belt, and the so-called high or flying kicks are **never** used. As for leg training (and this is true in most of the Gung Fu schools, North or South) it is not necessary for us to strengthen and toughen them by kicking on hard objects or sandbags. Due to their support of the whole body every day our legs already have power, and it is more a matter of cultivating them naturally. The training then involves the cultivating and concentrating of power, and the development of speed."

Gonnohyoe Yamamoto is the only two-time winner of the All-Japan All-Style Free-Fighting Championship. Here is what he had to say about the use of various techniques in combat:

"I won all my championships with <u>just a reverse punch and a front</u> <u>kick.</u>" In fact, he smiled: "The President of the Japanese Karate Association still talks about how I won the All-Japan All-Style Free-Fighting Championship with a down block to my opponent's blow, stepping in and scoring with a reverse punch. I have never used the fancy-dan techniques I've seen performed in America. I would say, in comparing an American Shodan with a Japanese First Degree, the American probably knows more techniques, but in general the Japanese can perform his fewer techniques in a much more efficient and better way.

"For instance, what does it matter if one can fly around the room if when he finally lands the other man gets him with a reverse punch? Let's face it. The best free-fighter is the man who scores even if he can't do all those acrobatic tricks. No one in his right mind would use them in a real fight. In Japan we would use only blows that would kill if not pulled."

"One of my techniques in free-fighting is to either punch or kick my opponents lead hand just hard enough to make that member useless for a second. Then, when his defense is made impotent, I step in and punch. Very basic, but I can testify to the fact that it is also very effective. In another one of my techniques I use my left hand to measure the distance between myself and my opponent and use my right hand to strike. While my left hand is distracting him I score with my right.

Now this is a technique anyone could use, even a White Belt, and he wouldn't have to be a circus acrobat to perform this quite effectively."

"What anyone needs is plenty of practice, repetitions of at least a couple of hundred times per day. I found shadow boxing was a very good way to master this technique. The most important single ingredient in being able to master a move of this sort is speed. Power comes later. The only way to develop speed, and eventually power, is by constant practice. That is why I, and other Japanese instructors, would rather make a student do 100,000 repetitions of a single technique than teach him a hundred new techniques, none of which he would be very effective with because he has not practiced them enough." "Of course", he smiled, "I've had opponents who jumped away when my left hand shot out and then struck instantly before I had a chance to get out."

"I never use a roundhouse kick or a back kick. In both of these a fighter leaves himself wide open and all an opponent has to do in either case is to jump forward, block the kick, and start punching. In the case of a back kick, a fighter is particularly vulnerable with a wide-open expanse of back, an enticing target for an opponent's punches. The same holds true for the wheel kick. It is not a move anyone would employ in a real karate match."

Where did these kicks originate? If they are useless in the context of a real-life fight, then why were they devised? Tae-Kwon-Do (Korean karate) has long been famous for its myriad kicks. I questioned Master Richard Chun on this subject:

"Since I had my parent's sanction I continued to practice and developed a very strong side kick. At that time in Korea, the only three kicks that had official approval were the side kick, the front kick, and the roundhouse kick. All others were frowned upon as being outside the art of Tae-Kwon-Do. I was watching ballet and noticed there were moves in it that were similar to the swing kick and the hook kick. Since these kicks are only about twenty years old, I wonder where these movements originated?"

The experts quoted above represent a wide variety of informed opinion on kicking techniques. The question still unanswered is: "Why the wide variety of useless leg maneuvers?".

I believe the key to this riddle is the American instructor's insatiable desire to teach new techniques. I feel that this is to keep the students interested so they don't quit. In Japan the instructor selects his students. An applicant for admission to a dojo in that country must first answer a number of questions pertaining to his character. If the answers after being analyzed are satisfactory, the applicant is then accepted for admission.

While he or she is a student the instructor watches for character defects, and also observes character development under the spiritual aspects of Budo training. It is almost impossible for a dishonest person or even a hot-head to reach Black Belt rank under such strict scrutiny and constant vigilance.

In America, on the other hand, anybody with the money to pay for lessons can select the instructor. The Sensei is therefore put in the same category as any other tradesman who has to try to please the customer. When I ask

American instructors why they are teaching in such-and-such a way they tell me this perpetual unveiling of tricks keeps their students happy! **Thus the origin of new movements.**

The very **practice** of karate should be enough to keep the student contented. Obviously everyone cannot be a karate person, just as everyone cannot be a physician, or an artist, or a master in any field that calls for intense discipline. People in karate who are bored by constant practice should simply not be in it. Karate is now enticing many people who are not suited to the rigorous self-control and patience needed to become even reasonably competent.

Americans tend to think that all Japanese are Black Belts, whereas the truth is, in that country out of every hundred who begin in karate only five make even Brown Belt. And out of that five only two or three will achieve Black Belt rank. It's a hard road, and teachers who attempt to ease the way are doing their students a disservice.   The American instructor who teaches many different techniques will amuse but will never train good karate persons. **If a student can perform one technique and perform it well, that is all he ever needs to do.**

CHAPTER EIGHTEEN

<u>I'M THE BAD GUY?</u>

The following account is a personal case history: Seeing the flash of the knife in the dark alley the young man jumped out of the way of the blade and tripped the knifer, sending him to the ground. He could feel the breath of a second mugger on his back, and whirling around smashed his nose with a back fist. When a third hood aimed a broken bottle at his face, he blocked and retaliated with a groin kick. A side kick to the stomach stopped a fourth attacker.

Suddenly he heard: "Put your hands up! We're the police!" The intended victim swung around with a grin of relief then froze as he noticed the police officer's gun pointed directly at **him**. For a second he had trouble understanding the command until it was repeated. The bore of the pistol made it effective, and he slowly raised his hands.

This true-life nightmare didn't end at the police station with the release of the young man. Instead he was held for arraignment and was released without bail. At the hearing, one of the arresting officers admitted that he had seen six men armed with knives and bottles attacking the young man. The Assistant District Attorney asked: "Then why did you arrest **him**?" The officer replied: "Because he was winning!"

This incident, which actually happened to me, and others like it that I know of, prove one dangerous point. Self-defense is not strictly legal. While it is true that eventually the charges may be dismissed there is no guarantee of this. Your defense attorney's fees are often astronomical.

Let's take a look at how the law reads. Quoting from Dewey Falcone's *"The Law And The Black Belt Holder"*: "We are entitled under the law to use that degree of force necessary under the circumstances to defend ourselves. If a deadly force is required you are entitled under the law to use deadly force. In most States there is a rule called "retreat to the wall". It states that if you are accosted and attacked anywhere you are required retreat until there is no place to go. Only then can you defend yourself. If some big fellow simply wises off at you, you cannot under any circumstances take physical action."

"However, if you are attacked with a deadly weapon than you, as a deadly-weapon yourself, may use whatever force is necessary. You may not, however, pursue your attacker and incapacitate or disarm them. If you do, you become the aggressor."

Another article, *"Crisis In Crime: The Law And You"* by Steve Smyser, deals more specifically with your legal right to self-defense. "First, it is very important to understand that you only have the right to stop the unlawful attack and to hold the attacker for the police. You do not have the right to beat the attacker after he has submitted, or to use unreasonable subduing force. You may only use equal force to overcome the force used against you."

Now can you imagine any situation where you have to stop after every split second to evaluate whether or not you are using "unreasonable force?".

Smyser continues: "If an attacker grabs you by the throat and applies only mild pressure you may only use enough force as is necessary to free yourself. The use of unreasonable force or a weapon makes you guilty of a criminal action. If someone standing well away from you threatens you with a knife he does not have the capability of completing the attack at that moment and legally you may not harm him in any way."

This means that in actual street-combat situations the legal rights of a martial-arts person to defend themselves are for all intents and purposes nonexistent. I know of a situation where a female student of mine pushed a man who was hitting her husband in the head with a baseball bat. The assailant fell and injured himself. The woman had to pay a huge attorney's fee to barely escape a felony conviction.

As I mentioned earlier, Preston Carter, a Fifth Dan Black Belt in karate, obeyed the legal restrictions and now is paralyzed with a bullet permanently lodged in his spine. From his hospital bed he told me: "In the case of the man with the knife, I should have made sure he wasn't able to attack me even if it meant breaking both of his arms. If I had it to do all over again and the man came at me armed with a weapon I would kill him. The same thing goes for those three other guys. If two men attack you even if they are unarmed go in to kill them. It's kill or be killed on the streets nowadays. That's what I tell my students even if they have to go to jail. It's better than ending up a paraplegic as I am now."

The law must be revised in light of today's increase in street violence. The right to realistic self-defense must be strongly reaffirmed by the law. The law-abiding citizen must be allowed the legal right to survive.

Many judges consider those with martial-arts training dangerous individuals who should be locked away. Sometimes in correctional institutions inmates who are martial artists are not allowed the same privileges as those of other athletes who participate in combative sports such as boxing and wrestling. A few years ago I received a letter from an inmate of Attica Prison. This man, who holds a Dan Rating (karate Black Belt) was not allowed to practice his art. He was not even allowed to receive martial arts publications! He asked me to appeal to the Warden to allow him to continue his training.

I interviewed one well-known instructor on the subject of legality: "Legal! There's nothing legal about somebody taking my life or that of a family member. In a street mugging the attacker doesn't care whether you are a Black Belt. All he knows is that he wants your money and he's willing to hurt you for it. In a situation like that it is either kill or be killed. Whatever weapon the person attacked has he or she should use it on the attacker to save their own life. The rule is: "**DO IT FIRST!**"

APPENDIX ONE

MARTIAL ARTS MEDIA RESOURCES

The rise of the internet has forced many traditional print magazines to cease publication. The costs involved in printing and distributing magazines simply cannot be offset through advertising revenue in this highly competitive arena. Kung Fu Magazine is among others that have been forced to close after many years of publication. The following alphabetical lists are the better known print and online offerings available today:

PRINT MEDIA

Black Belt Magazine: blackbeltmag.com (monthly)

Jiu-Jitsu Magazine: jiujitsumag.com (6x/year)

Ultimate MMA Magazine: ultimatemmamag.com (monthly)

Journal of Martial Arts: goviamedia.com (3x/year)

Kung Fu Tai Chi Magazine: kungfumagazine.com (6x/year)

Tai Chi: tai-chi.com (a 4-page newsletter)

WWE Magazine: wwe.com/magazine (monthly)

ON-LINE MEDIA

Action Martial Arts Magazine: actionmagstore.com

Bushido Online Magazine: bushido-online.com

Combat Canada: combatcanada.ca

Electronic Journal of Martial Arts and Sciences (EJMAS): lists 13 online journals: ejmas.com

Fight Times: fighttimes.com

Martial Arts Central:
martialartscentral.com

Martial Arts – Show Biz TV: martialarts-showbiztv.com

Martial Edge: martialedge.com

Martial Force: martialforce.com

Shiai Magazine: shiaimagazine.net

Taekwondo Times:
taekwondotimes.com

The Way of Taekwondo: ataonline.com

Truwaza Martial Arts Times:
truwaza.weebly.com

Wing Chun Teahouse: ocwingchun.com

APPENDIX TWO

MARTIAL ARTS ORGANIZATIONS

There are over two-hundred (!) martial arts organizations worldwide listed at:

www.dmoz.org/sports/martial_arts/organizations

A few of the best-known groups are listed below, in no particular order:

World Professional Martial Arts Organization (Founder/Director Great Grand Master Aaron Banks)

www.sites.google.com/site/martialartswpmao/

World Karate Federation: wkf.net

Funakoshi Shotokan Karate Association: fska.com

World Martial Arts Association: wmaa.org

United States Martial Arts Association (USMAA):

wwmaa.org

American Martial Art Association: amorg.com

The American Kempo Karate Association: torakendo.com

Aikido Association of America: aaa-aikido.com

Aikido Association of North America: doshinkan-aikido.org

Aikido Institute of America: aikidoinstitute.com

International Karate Alliance: karatealliance.com

International Karate Association: ikakarate.com

Professional Karate Commission: phcheadquarters.org

International Judo Federation: intjudo.eu

American Center For Chinese Studies: kungfu.org

World Taekwondo Foundation: wtf.org

American Ju-Jitsu Association: americanjujitsuassociation.org

United States Ju-Jitsu Federation: usjjf.org

American Hapkido Federation: ushapkido.com

International Disabled Self-Defense Association: defenseability.com

GLOSSARY OF

MARTIAL ARTS TERMS

The following glossary is far from a complete description of all martial arts terms, which in total could comprise a small dictionary! There are a vast number of terms used in China, Japan, Korea, Thailand, Burma, India and the Philippines that are seldom used in America. Nor does this glossary list all of the many different weapons found throughout martial arts disciplines. Nor does it go back in time to the days of the Shaolin Temple and the Ninja warriors. It is intended to provide an insight into some of the more common martial arts terminology heard in America today and used throughout the book.

AIKIDO - Japanese martial art invented by Morehei Ueshiba. It involves internal and external harmony with nature. The techniques of this system are circular in movement.

ATEMI - Japenese art of attacking the

vital points of the body. It is used in jiu jitsu, but is illegal in judo contests.

BANDO - Burmese martial art involving numerous boxing methods. It is based upon twelve animals, which are the Boar, Bull, Cobra, Deer, Eagle, Monkey, Bird, Panther, Python, Scorpion, Tiger and Viper. It was introduced into the west by Dr. Maung Gyi in 1962.

BLACK BELT - Belt representing the first significant rank in the martial arts training. Achieving this level of proficiency allows one to teach the art to others. In the Japanese ranking system it is known as Shodan.

BOKKEN - Solid wooden sword used for training purposes in kendo and other martial arts. In the hands of an expert it can deliver fatal blows.

BOK MEI PAI - White Eyebrow, style of kung fu, named after it's founder, Bok Mei. It is a very fast style of kung fu, which legend states to have been banned at the Shaolin temple after Bok

Mei killed a fellow student in a fight.

BUDO – A Japanese martial art.

CENTER LINE - Basic theory of Wing Chun Kung Fu, in which students are taught to defend and attack an imaginary line running down the center of the body on which all vital organs are located.

CHI - Internal energy, the universal force which is harnessed through a series of special breathing exercises called Chi-Kung or Gung.

CHI SAO - Special exercise in Wing Chun Kung Fu for developing coordination and sensitivity in the arms. It is also very important for teaching correct elbow positioning and economy of motion. It is known in the west as Sticking Hands.

CHUAN-FA - Chinese term meaning Way of the Fist. This is the correct term for Kung Fu.

CHUDAN - In Japanese Martial Arts the middle area or chest. In Karate this is one of the three target areas of the body.

DAISENSEI – A title of respect, meaning "Great Teacher", given only to an instructor of high rank.

DAITO-RYU - Style of Aiki Jutsu from which it is said that Aikido developed.

DAN - Japanese term for anyone who has achieved the rank of Black Belt or above.

DIM MAK - Fabled death touch, a delayed action strike aimed at an acupuncture meridian, able to cause death to a victim within hours or days of its delivery.

DO - Japanese word for "Path" or "Way Of". It is used at the end of the name of a martial art, as in Karate Do or Kendo.

DOJO - Training place, used for the

practice of Martial Arts.

DRUNKEN MONKEY - Style of Kung Fu based upon the antics of monkeys. Practitioners stagger around as though intoxicated to fool their opponents.

ELBOW - Close quarter weapon used in almost all martial arts systems. It is of particular interest to the Muay Thai fighters of Thailand.

EMPTY HAND - Literal the meaning of "Karate" in Japanese.

FIVE ANIMALS - Five animals, the Crane, Dragon, Leopard, Tiger and Snake, whose movements were imitated in a system of fighting said to be the origin of the earliest martial arts systems.

FORM – A series of choreographed movements in Kung Fu linking together various martial arts techniques, able to be performed as a solo exercise to aid the practitioner in perfecting his technique. The equivalent in Karate is called a Kata.

<u>FU JOW PAI</u> - Tiger Claw system of Kung Fu.

<u>FULL CONTACT</u> - Form of Karate in which full power kicks are delivered at an opponent. Participants wear protective hand and foot equipment. The sport has grown rapidly in western countries in recent years.

<u>GEDAN</u> - Lower area of the body, from the wait downwards, in Japanese Martial Arts.

<u>GI</u> - Term used for the training uniform worn in Martial Arts. It is known as a Karate Gi in Karate and Judo Gi in Judo.

<u>GOJU KAI</u> – Martial arts style created by Gogen Yamaguchi. It incorporates circular and linear movements.

<u>GUNG FU</u> - Cantonese pronunciation of Kung Fu.

HACHIDAN - An 8th degree Black Belt, Hachi means Eight. In Japanese Martial Arts the title denotes a professor of the art.

HADAN - Taekwondo term for the area of the body below the waist, equivalent to the Japanese "Gedan".

HAKAMA – The long divided-skirt-garment covering the legs and feet, used in Kendo, Aikido and other Japanese Martial Arts. The long robe is said to mask the intricate footwork of the practitioner, thereby making it difficult for an opponent to judge his movements.

HAPKIKO - Korean Martial Art involving many difficult kicks, but also utilizing locks and holds. It is somewhat similar to the Japanese Aikido.

HOMBU - Headquarters of any Martial Art.

HOP GAR – A style of Kung Fu which became prominent during the Ching

Dynasty of China. It was famous as the official martial art of the Manchu Emperors. The two distinct styles within the system were, White Crane and Law Horn. The style is also known by the name Lama Kung Fu.

HUNG GAR – A style of Kung Fu stressing powerful hand techniques delivered from low stances. It is based on the movements of the Tiger and Crane. It is one of the original five ancestor styles. Hung is the creator's name and Gar means Family or System.

HYUNG – A pattern of solo practice movements in Taekwondo, similar to a "Form" in Kung Fu and a "Kata" in Karate.

IAI-DO - Japanese method of drawing a sword and re-sheathing it. Thiiis is a non-combat art aimed at leading the practitioner to intellectual and spiritual awareness. John McGee was trained in Iai-do.

INTERNAL SYSTEMS - There are three internal styles of Kung Fu: Tai Chi, Pakua and Hsing 1. They each cultivate chi energy, an inherent power within all human beings, largely inexplicable to modern science, which can be unleashed to awesome effect.

IPPON - Full point awarded in Martial Arts competitions for the flawless execution of a technique.

IRON PALM - Lethal technique of Kung Fu, able to kill with a single blow. The entire forearm must be conditioned over a period of several years before a practitioner is able to attain any reasonable standard. This conditioning makes the adept's hand and arm as an iron bar.

ISSHIN RYU – A Japanese martial art (kusarigamajutsu) that employs the chain and the scythe.

JEET KUNE DO - Style of Kung Fu devised by the late Bruce Lee. Its name means "Way of the Intercepting Fist".

JKA - Japan Karate Association, founded in 1955. It is the largest karate association in the world. Its first chief instructor was the founder of Shotokan, Gichin Funakoshi.

JKI JITSU - Japanese Martial Art based upon the exploitation of opponents strength against himself. The name means Soft or Flexible. The art contains both armed an unarmed techniques.

JODAN - In Japanese Martial Arts the top area of the body, from the shoulders upward.

JUDO - Modern sporting form of Jiu Jitsu, developed by Dr. Jigoro Kano in 1882.

JUDOKA - One who practices Judo.

JU-JITSU or JIU-JITSU – Jiu = gentle or flexible; Jitsu = art. A method developed in Japan of defending oneself without the use of weapons by using the strength and weight of an adversary to disable him.

KARATEKA – One who practices karate.

KATA - A prescribed series of repetitious karate moves meant for solo practice to improve skills.

KALI (and KIA) - Super shout or yell in Japanese Martial Arts, emitted when applying a technique to add extra power and stun an opponent.

KIHON - Basic training moves, repeated many times in order to reach proficiency.

KUMITE – A martial arts tournament.

KUNG FU - A derivative of a Chinese term meaning "Hard Work and Applied Skills", accepted by both Westerners and Orientals as a generic term for martial art skills.

KUP - In Taekwondo one of the eight grades of ranking before the Black Belt.

KYO KUSHIN KAI - Japanese Karate System founded by the Korean born Mastau Oyama. Its name means "Way of Ultimate Truth". Oyama gained fame by fighting bulls barehanded. He still holds the world record for breaking the largest number of roofing tiles with one blow.

LO HAN - The name of the exercises that were taught to the ancient temple monks when found in an emaciated condition. The method of training known as "The 18 hands of the Lo Han" and is the basis of what we now know as Kung Fu.

MAKIWARA - Striking post or board used to condition the hands and feet in karate.

MARTIAL ARTS - A term denoting the arts of war, derived from "mars", the god of war. It now means any fighting discipline designed to promote combat proficiency.

MOOK JOONG - Wooden dummy, shaped like a man, used for conditioning and training purposes in many styles of Kung Fu.

NINJA - Secret society of highly trained assassins in old Japan, trained from birth to become expert in a vast number of martial skills.

NUNCHAKU - Two wooden batons linked by a short chain or cord to make an awesome weapon. Used originally as a rice flail, it is found in most cultures throughout Asia.

PA-KUA - Style of Kung Fu, based on circular movements with open palm strikes. It means Eight Trigrams and the concept comes from the classic Chinese treatise, the *I-Ching*, or book of changes. The practitioner constantly changes directions during an attack. Because of this the art is sometimes known as "Eight-Directions Palm

Boxing".

PRAYING MANTIS - Style of Kung Fu known in China as Ton Long. It is named after Wong Long, who invented the style after witnessing a fight between a grasshopper and a praying mantis.

RYU - School or Style in Japanese Martial Arts.

SAMBO – A Russian martial art. Acronym for Samooborona Bez Oruzhiya , which translates as "self-defense without weapons".

SAMURAI - Japanese feudal warrior. The word means "one who serves". A samurai served as a military retainer to a Lord and his shogun. A masterless samurai was known as a Ronin.

SANCHIN – The three internal battles of "body", "mind" and "Spirit".

SENSEI - Japanese word of respect for

a teacher or instructor.

SHAOLIN - Temple in the Songshan mountains of northern China, where Kung Fu is said to have born.

SHIATSU – Accupressure therapy based on putting pressure on specific body energy points.

SHODAN – The lowest Black Belt rank.

SHORIN-JI RYU – A form of Okinawan karate.

SHOTOKAN - School of Japanese Karate founded by Gichin Funakoshi. It is probably the most widely practiced style of Karate in the world.

SHURIKEN - Sharp pointed throwing stars, originally made of iron, a favorite weapon of the Ninja. Many shapes and sizes exist.

SHUTO – A sharp chop with the side of the hand.

SIFU - Instructor in Kung Fu,

corresponding to a Sensei in Karate. The word means Father.

SPORT KARATE - Karate competition in which contestants fight under combat rules in a ring or area. They wear protective gloves and foot pads. Techniques are scored and points are given.

TAEKWONDO - Korean style of empty hand combat very similar to Karate. Great emphasis is placed upon delivering strikes with the feet and fists. This art was partly indigenous to Korea, being known as Tae Dyon in its original version.

TAI CHI CHUAN - One of the three internal systems of Kung Fu. Much value is placed upon its therapeutic properties for the relief of stress and tension. It is intended to guide one into a state of peace and tranquility. The word means "Great Ultimate Fist".

TAMASHIWARA - Japanese technique of using strikes with the body against materials such as wood, tiles, bricks and ice to test the power of a strike.

TANG SOO DO - Way of the Tang Hand, a Korean Martial Art System very similar to Japanese Shotokan Karate.

TAO - Chinese term meaning Path or Way. Tao is an invisible force or energy, present in all things in the universe.

TOBOK - Suit or Tunic worn by practitioners of Taekwondo, consisting of a loose shirt and trousers tied in the middle with a sash or belt.

VITAL POINTS - Certain areas on the body which, when struck in a particular way, cause great pain or death.

WADO RYU KARATE - Way of Peace, style of Japanese Karate developed from Shotokan by Hironori Ohtsuka.

WAZARI - In competitive martial arts a score of half a point, awarded to the skillful execution of a technique.

WHITE BELT - Color of belt to a beginner in most Japanese Martial Arts.

WING CHUN - Chinese Martial Art invented by a woman named Wing Chun. Its name means "Beautiful Springtime". It is considered by many to be one of the most effective forms of Kung Fu in existence. The fundamental premise of the style is economy of motion. Wing Chun greatly influenced Bruce Lee when he was formulating his personal system of Jeet Kune Do.

YANG - In Chinese cosmology the positive aspect of the universe relating to hardness, masculinity and light, one half of the Taoist view of the universe.

YAWARA STICK – A six-inch long tubular stick held within the fist with ends projecting from each side, used in self-defense by chopping or poking at an adversary.

YIN - In Chinese cosmology, the negative aspect of the universe, relating to emptiness, softness, darkness and femininity. Yin is represented as a black fish with a white eye in the famous Yin-Yang symbol.

YODAN – A 4th Degree Black Belt.

YUDANSHA – A Kendoka who has achieved the rank of Black Belt or higher, alone permitted to wear an outfit of a uniform color.

ZEN - Religious philosophy that claims that one can reach satori, or enlightenment, through meditation. Founded by the Indian Monk and Holy Man Bodhidharma,   Zen makes use of paradoxical poems called Koans to clear the mind of trivia.